To the hard-working *picanteras* and chefs in traditional restaurants in the Andes of Peru, and to the brilliant Vitelio Reyes, Ana Velazquez and Miguel Arbe who have contributed greatly to this book with recipes. To Raquel de Oliveira and all our family at Andina and Casita Andina, and to my amazing wife Lucy and kids Felix and Otilia, whose support and love make every day so special.

MARTIN MORALES

ANDINA

The heart of Peruvian food

RECIPES AND STORIES
FROM THE ANDES

FOOD PHOTOGRAPHY BY DAVID LOFTUS
REPORTAGE PHOTOGRAPHY BY DAVE BROWN

quadrille

LONDON PUBLIC LIBRARY

Publishing Director: Sarah Lavelle
Creative Director: Helen Lewis
Designer: Dave Brown (apeinc.co.uk)
Project Editor: Judy Barratt
Recipe Editor: Catherine Phipps
Studio Recipe Photographer: David Loftus
Reportage Photographer: Dave Brown (davebrownphoto.com)
Food Stylist: Pip Spence
Prop Stylist: Vic Allen
Calligrapher and Map Illustrator: Sarah Locher
Story Illustrator: Shila Acosta
Production: Vincent Smith and Tom Moore

First published in 2017 by Quadrille Publishing,
Pentagon House, 52–54 Southwark Street, London SE1 1UN
www.quadrille.co.uk
Quadrille is an imprint of Hardie Grant

www.hardiegrant.com.au

Notes on the recipes
Unless otherwise specified, use:
Medium free-range or organic eggs
Fresh herbs
Medium-sized vegetables
Whole-fat dairy products
Unwaxed lemons
Salted butter

Medium-heat red chillies are chillies such as red serenade or caldero.
For a speedier alternative to panca and amarillo chilli pastes and to rocoto pepper paste,
try PK Peruvian Kitchen Sauces. More details on page 270.
A list of suppliers of Andina ingredients appears on page 270.

Source organic, free-range meat whenever you can, and use fish from sustainable sources.

Oven temperatures are for a fan-assisted oven.
Use metric or imperial measurements, not a mixture of the two.

CONTENTS

Andina, a word meaning a woman, or a dish or ingredient from the Andes. My grandmother Mamita Naty, my mum and my great aunts were all Andinas. I have Andina in my blood.

WHY ANDINA?

Even though I grew up in the coastal city of Lima, with its culinary influences coming from all four corners of Peru and from immigrants from as far as Spain, Italy, Africa, China and Japan, reminders of my Andina heritage were all around me as a child. My great aunts (with whom I stayed at weekends) and their cooking, the food parcels Mamita Naty would send me every month, and the Andina traditions we followed in Lima built for me a cultural landscape that was alive and fascinating. The more I experienced it, the more I fell in love with it. Despite enjoying and learning about the different aspects of Peruvian food, I always returned to the centre, the starting point, the most ancient aspect of our cuisine. That's Andina cuisine. So for me, Andina is a world full of food and stories too precious to remain unspoken; it is *la cocina Andina*, the cuisine of the Andes, the heart of Peruvian food.

Andina cuisine is always perfectly balanced and seasonal. If it's summer, Andina cooking offers us the lightest and zestiest dishes; if it's winter, the dishes are warming, hearty and filling. Using ingredients that are both seasonal and local, and a wide variety of ancient cooking techniques, this cuisine is built upon respect for the environment, the land and its people. As the highly respected Peruvian sociologist and gastronomy writer Isabel Álvarez says, 'This is not fashionable food, this is food from thousands of years ago.' Since ancient times it has been organic, nose-to-tail eating, from field to table with zero waste. In this way, ancient it might be, but it is also progressive.

Andina cooking is a perfect example of how a cuisine can evolve and adapt. Some ingredients, dishes and drinks date back thousands of years; others immigrants brought with them within the last five centuries. But there are others, such as recipes we have created in our restaurants and for this book, that might be a matter of only years or months old. The book includes examples of all these, ultimately harking back to the energy and creativity of the real stars of Peruvian cuisine: the *picanteras*, the generations of Andina women chefs, who are the purveyors of the great flavours and techniques that are so unique to my country's gastronomy.

It's easy to fall into the trap of thinking that the more complicated or elaborate we make something, the better it will be. Often, all we need is something simple. For me, Andina cuisine offers that perspective. For the last 30 years, I have travelled the length and breadth of the Andes researching ingredients, tasting traditional recipes and spending time with the *picanteras*. I have eaten in their *picanterías* and in hundreds of other wonderful restaurants high in the Andes. Their dishes shy away from complexity and over-preparation. They are practical and economical, and yet they deliver a vast array of flavour.

I share something very personal with the *picanteras*. Many lost their mothers at a young age and had to find a trade, feed themselves and their siblings and learn that special seasoning touch, which in Peru we call *sazón*. So did I. When my mother moved out when I was ten years old, I was left to cook for my dad and sister. I can't live without eating great food; I crave deliciousness, ideally in good company. Now, like so many Andina women I admire, I work in restaurants spending my days feeding beautiful, wholesome food to happy, hungry people.

REGIONAL COOKING IN THE ANDES

The Andes spans seven South American countries: Peru, Bolivia, Ecuador, Argentina, Chile, Colombia and Venezuela. The Peruvian Andes alone is made up of eleven different Andina regions (see p.208), each with its own traditional cuisine with ancient and modern influences, as well as its own geography, flora, fauna, climate and cultural identity.

In the Andes, generation after generation, people have communicated through music, dance, rituals and, above all, through food and drink. There is no significant activity that does not involve food: from weddings to saints' celebrations, births to deaths, festivals to indigenous rituals. Celebration and ritual food might be slightly more complex, using techniques that can take a little longer, but day-to-day cooking is practical, quick and nutritious: starters are soups and broths and a main is usually a *picante*, a kind of stew. Farmers have *el fiambre*, hearty packed lunches to last all day. And family meals are built around the most accessible ingredients – tubers and cereals – adding vegetables, meats and cheeses, if available. Above all, though, traditional Andina cooking uses no industrialized processes. Andina cooks use wood-burning stoves and open fires, and centuries-old manual implements, such as the batán millstone (see p.41). There is even underground *pachamanca* cooking at special occasions (see p.109). The cooking also features pre-Hispanic techniques for flavouring, preserving or transforming ingredients. Among them are specific ways to smoke, dry, infuse, marinate and ferment. From goat to alpaca, beef to lamb, potatoes to cheeses, coffee to spirits, the Andina women have found ways to flavour, cook and preserve everything the land and rivers give them.

The Andes is a mixture of urban and rural environments. There are large, busy cities that share traits with cities everywhere (migration, transportation and technology – all of which have evolved the Andina way of life, including its food), relatively uninhabited highlands, and most of all many farming communities. Here, people unite in the kitchen, as they have done for thousands of years, around pots and pans. Women, who are mostly responsible for the cooking, are at the heart of home life. Many

also manage the selling of produce that comes from their farms. The ancient barter system, known as *trueque*, encourages fair commerce among indigenous farmers and their communities. These exchanges value generosity: fruit, vegetable, meat and fish sellers always agree a deal with their customers, but offer a considerate little extra, called *la yapa*, on top.

Ancient peoples living in the Andes created sophisticated methods of farming, many of which are still in use today – from expertly managing agriculture at 4,000 metres above sea level to building complex irrigation systems and levelled platforms, called *andenes*, to ensure a measured water supply for crops. There are an estimated 2,000 varieties of indigenous potatoes; enormous quantities of seeds and grains, such as quinoa, amaranth and *cañigua* among them; as well as unique fruit such as lucuma, beans such as El Pajuro, and herbs such as *muña*, *chincho* and *huacatay*. With the Spanish came cucumber and limes, among other fruit and vegetables, as well as herbs and cereals. They brought goats, sheep and cows to join the native rabbit, guinea pig, duck, pheasant and llama. Having already taken over parts of Central America, the Spanish also brought cacao, vanilla and prickly pear fruit; while ingredients such as palms, banana and cassava came from Africa as a result of the slave trade. The influx of Asians in the 19th century brought tamarind and ginger, as well as rice; while in the 20th century, migrants from Austria and Germany have given us the techniques and flavours of northern Europe. The result is a rich melting pot of culinary influences, all of which fascinate and excite me and inspire the chefs in our restaurants.

ANDINA AND CASITA ANDINA RESTAURANTS

I often say to my team, if a dish has been around for a thousand years, it has survived for a reason. Crafted over time at the hands of many cooks and chefs, it has fought off trends, fads and other challenges by evolving and adapting but never losing its essence and great flavour. At our award-winning restaurants in London, our dishes are inspired by these traditional soul-food dishes, made using the best possible ingredients and always beautifully presented.

I like to think of our design and service in a similar way. Andina is a kind of sanctuary: calm and comfortable in the daytime, buzzing at night; a modern-day *picantería* in London with a team of people who really love what they do. It has an open kitchen with counter eating so that our guests can chat with our chefs, a pisco bar and a juice bar, and a music room featuring a collection of more than 1,000 vinyl singles of Peruvian music. The food and architecture are inspired by the regions of La Libertad (see p.214) and Arequipa (p.218). When we first opened, the idea of it seemed almost too alien for people: 'A *picantería* in the middle of East London? What's that?' But soon, happy locals discovered it and so did many chefs, intrigued by our work.

At Casita Andina (meaning 'little Andina house') we are inspired by the food of Cusco, Ayacucho, and of Huancayo in Junín (see pp.238–42, 227–31 and 250–55). It is a cosy, charming *picantería* with commissioned art from the regions' artisan craftsmakers and contemporary painters, telling our stories and paying homage to our food, our *picanteras* and our traditions.

ABOUT THIS BOOK

Andina is by no means a complete cookbook on the cuisine of the Peruvian Andes; nor is it a 'restaurant cookbook' in the strictest sense of the term. It's my creative expression of both, and offers more than that, too. This is a cookbook complemented with stories that bring meaning and life to our recipes and to the Andina regions.

About half of the recipes are selected key dishes from the eleven regions of the Peruvian Andes; in the other half, we have created new recipes that are influenced by the ingredients and traditions of those regions. We serve both kinds in our restaurants, as food should be made from what you have available. Sometimes we use native Andina ingredients, but in this book we have made sure always to offer alternative local ingredients, if needed. So, ours is a cuisine that is accessible to a home chef (you can buy the ingredients at your local supermarket and not necessarily just in the most obscure market high up in the Andes), but with flavours that you will relish and techniques that will surprise you. In a way, in this book, we are bringing you new colours and paintbrushes, and now the canvas is yours to paint.

ANDINA STORIES

At the end of the book are eleven stories, one for each region, that form the backdrop to the recipes; they are an expression of my very personal relationship with the Andina regions. Through my travels I've met farmers and women produce sellers at many markets, and I've cooked with wonderful *picanteras*. These Andina women drive us forward,

encouraging us to explore, evolve, challenge and refine our cooking. This book gives a voice to those unsung heroes; it is a clear acknowledgement of the magnitude of the Andinas' contribution to Peruvian food. It is both an expression of my gratitude to them and a celebration of their work for you.

The Andina regions of Peru also provide so much worldly significance in terms of terrain and history, such as the deepest canyon, the highest lake, the longest mountain range, one of the most advanced ancient civilizations and some of the most nutritious and unique ingredients on the planet. This is a majestic landscape of gods and battles, of humility and oppression, of exploitation and survival, of stunning geographical beauty – a beauty and a land that has inspired chefs and cooks, as well as photographers, painters, musicians and writers since time immemorial. This is the land that the Inca Túpac Amaru was sacrificed for, the great José María Arguedas eloquently wrote about, the photographer Martín Chambi chronicled so beautifully. It is the land that José Sabogal painted, Daniel Alomía Robles translated through harmonies, Flor Pucarina sings about, and gave birth to Mario Vargas Llosa, winner of the Nobel Prize in Literature.

This energy and creativity is how I see Andina. I'm married to this vast region and its people through my work and our restaurants, and I'm thrilled you can join me in celebrating it in this book.

Desayunos

BREAKFASTS

Picante de Huevos

SERVES 4

Fiery Eggs. *If you want a dish to really wake you up and give you oomph for the day ahead, this recipe does the trick. It's a firm brunch favourite at Andina, with people coming from far and wide to try it.*

1 tbsp olive oil

1 red onion, finely chopped

2 garlic cloves, crushed

2 tbsp panca chilli paste (see below)

1 tbsp amarillo chilli paste (see below)

2 red peppers, deseeded and diced

3 tomatoes, deseeded and very finely sliced

1 tbsp tomato purée

4 eggs

50g Cheddar cheese, grated

2 spring onions, finely sliced

4 coriander sprigs, leaves roughly chopped, plus a few whole

Slices of toast, to serve (optional)

Salt and ground black pepper

For the panca chilli paste (makes about 30ml)

2 dried panca chillies

For the amarillo chilli paste (makes about 100ml)

1 tbsp olive oil

¼ onion, finely chopped

2 garlic cloves, finely chopped

2 amarillo chillies, or 2 medium-heat red chillies and ½ yellow pepper, deseeded and finely chopped

First, make the chilli pastes. For the panca chilli paste, cover the dried chillies in water and soak for 2 hours. Drain, then blitz with a stick blender, add salt to taste and set aside until needed.

While the panca chillies are soaking, make the amarillo chilli paste. Heat the oil in a small frying pan over a low–medium heat. Fry the onion for 7–8 minutes until soft, but not browned, then add the garlic and chilli (or alternative) and fry for 2–3 minutes more to soften. Season with salt to taste, then allow to cool completely. When cool, blitz to a smooth paste, then set aside until needed. (You can store any leftover in an airtight container the fridge for up to 1 week.)

Heat the olive oil in a large, ovenproof frying pan or shallow casserole. Add the onion and sauté over a low heat for 7–8 minutes until slightly softened, then add the garlic and chilli pastes and cook for a further 2–3 minutes until the garlic has softened but not taken on any colour. Season well with salt and pepper.

Add the red pepper, tomato and tomato purée, and stir to combine. Cover with a lid and simmer over a low heat for 5 minutes until the peppers have softened and the sliced tomatoes have collapsed down, then remove the lid and allow the sauce to reduce for 3–4 minutes until most of the liquid has evaporated. Use a ladle to spoon half the mixture into a food processor or blender and blitz until smooth, then return it to the pan and stir to combine.

Use the back of a tablespoon to make 4 indentations in the vegetable mixture and break an egg into each hollow. Cover the pan and leave it on the stovetop for 5 minutes to cook the eggs.

Remove from the heat and sprinkle with Cheddar cheese, chopped spring onion and the chopped and whole coriander leaves, and serve with slices of toast on the side, if you wish.

Otongo

SERVES 4

Sweet Steamed Potato Buns. *I've stuffed these buns with sugar and topped them with almonds and smoked bacon, but you could replace the bacon with dried fruits for a vegetarian version, or leave out the sugar and make them only savoury using pork crackling, pancetta, ham or cheese. The brilliant Andina chef Pamela Rojas taught me this dish after I spotted it in Huancayo's main market.*

300g plain flour, plus extra for kneading

1 tsp fast-action dried yeast

1 tsp baking powder

1 tsp granulated sugar

½ tsp salt

50g cooled mashed potato

150ml full-fat milk

50g yacon syrup or muscovado sugar

2 corns-on-the-cob, stripped of their green husks, husks reserved

50g flaked almonds, crushed, to serve

2 slices of smoked bacon, fried until crisp and crumbled, to serve

Put the flour, yeast, baking powder and granulated sugar in a large bowl and mix thoroughly. Add the salt, then crumble in the potato. Put the milk in a small pan over a low heat and warm through slightly, then gradually work it into the dry ingredients until you have a sticky dough. Turn out the dough and knead it on a floured surface until it becomes smooth and elastic, then return it to the bowl, cover with a damp cloth and allow it to rise for 2 hours until doubled in size.

When the dough has doubled, remove it from the bowl to a floured surface, pull, fold and knead it to knock it back until completely smooth. Cut the dough into 8 portions and shape each portion into a round. Push your thumb into the centre of each round, almost to the bottom, to make a well. Spoon a little yacon syrup or muscovado sugar into each well and bring the dough together over the top to seal. Cover the buns with a damp cloth and allow to prove for at least 30 minutes.

Put the buns in a large steamer – you will probably have to do this in two batches: place the stripped corn cobs in the steaming water (this is to create height in the steamer), line the steaming basket with the husks and place the buns on top. Steam the buns for about 15–20 minutes until well risen and springy to touch. To serve, sprinkle with the crushed almonds and crumbled bacon, then tear apart while still warm and eat just as they are.

Note: You can strip the steamed corn cobs of their kernels, allow to cool and keep in an airtight container in the fridge for up to 3 days. Reheat in a frying pan with a little melted butter until caramelized and serve as a side veg for lunch or supper.

Tamal de Sabogal

SERVES 4

Sabogal's Tamal. *Making a tamal requires craft and creativity, so this recipe is named after José Sabogal, the painter and muralist, who was born in Cajamarca, a place known for its great tamales. We usually use the Andina choclo corn (pictured) for this recipe, but sweetcorn works well, too. The combination of sweet and savoury, with a runny egg yolk, cured salmon and herby hollandaise, is mouthwatering.*

60g granulated sugar

60g salt, plus extra to season

½ bunch of dill, finely chopped

50g panca chilli powder, or chipotle or other smoked chilli powder

600g salmon fillet, skinned

4 poached eggs, to serve

Freshly ground black pepper

For the tamales

50–75g cornmeal

450g cooked sweetcorn kernels, puréed

100ml full-fat milk

8 corn husks, soaked in warm water for 20 minutes, then drained

For the huacatay hollandaise

A bunch of huacatay, or a small bunch each of coriander, tarragon and mint

6 parsley sprigs

250g unsalted butter

4 egg yolks

Juice of ½ lime

First, make the salmon cure. Mix the sugar, salt, dill and chilli powder together. Rub this into the salmon, making sure both sides of the fish are well covered. Put the fish in a plastic self-seal bag, or lay it out on a small tray and cover with clingfilm, then refrigerate for 48 hours, turning every few hours when you can.

To make the sweetcorn tamales, mix 50g of cornmeal with the puréed sweetcorn, milk and a generous pinch of salt. You should have a thick, spreadable paste – if the mixture is a little loose, add another 25g of cornmeal and mix again. Divide the mixture equally between the 8 corn husks and fold each husk to form a square parcel, making it as secure as possible to keep in the filling. Put the husks in a steamer and cook for 25 minutes. Remove from the steamer and allow to stand – they will firm up as they cool.

While the husks cool, make the hollandaise. Place all the herbs in a food processor or blender with a little water and blitz to a smooth purée. Put the butter in a small saucepan over a low heat and allow it to melt very gently. When it has melted, remove from the heat and set aside. In a bowl, whisk the egg yolks with half the lime juice, then gradually whisk in the melted butter until it emulsifies and you have a rich, creamy sauce. Stir in the herb purée and season with salt and pepper. Taste and add a little more lime juice if you think it needs it. Keep the hollandaise warm until you are ready to serve (if you need to reheat it, just take care that it doesn't start to bubble).

To assemble the dish, open the tamales but leave them on the corn husks – use 2 per person. Rinse the salmon thoroughly to remove the cure, then slice it thinly on the diagonal. Place a few slices of salmon on top of each tamale, top with the poached eggs, then drizzle over some of the hollandaise. Serve the remaining hollandaise at the table.

Granola de los Andes

SERVES 4

Granola Andina. *The Peruvian Andes is home to a wide variety of nutritious grains and seeds – I've brought some of them together in my favourite combo here, but feel free to mix and match. This dish has it all: I love the crunch, and the sour, fruity and spicy flavours.*

200g rolled oats

25g uncooked white quinoa

25g uncooked red quinoa

2 tbsp cañigua or chia seeds

100g pecans, roughly chopped

75g flaked almonds

75g shredded coconut

60g pumpkin seeds

½ tsp ground cinnamon

A pinch of salt

100g yacon or maple syrup

75g coconut oil

1 tsp vanilla extract

For the physalis coulis

50g physalis, roughly chopped

50g granulated sugar or yacon syrup

For the amaranth pop

2 tsp amaranth

To serve

10g maca powder (optional)

300g Greek yogurt

A few strawberries, hulled and halved

A handful of blueberries or blackberries

Preheat the oven to 150°C (gas mark 2). Line a baking tray with nonstick baking parchment.

Make the granola. Mix all the dry ingredients together in a large bowl. Gently heat the syrup and coconut oil together in a small saucepan with the vanilla, over a low heat. When the syrup and oil have melted, pour the mixture over the dry ingredients and mix thoroughly.

Spread the granola mix over the lined baking tray as evenly as possible. Put it in the oven and bake for 50–60 minutes, stirring once or twice for even browning, until golden brown. Remove the tray from the oven and cover with baking parchment. Place another baking tray on top and weigh it down with a couple of tins – this will help compact the granola and glue it together. Allow to cool, then transfer it to an airtight container.

To make the coulis, put the fruit and the sugar or syrup with a splash of water in a small saucepan over a low heat. Heat gently until the syrup or sugar has melted, then increase the heat and simmer until the mixture has reduced to a viscous consistency (about 4–5 minutes).

To make the amaranth pop, heat a small saucepan over a medium heat. Add the amaranth and cover with a lid. After a few seconds the amaranth should start popping. Wait until the popping subsides, then remove from the heat immediately and set aside.

To serve, whisk the maca powder, if using, with the yogurt until well combined. Divide the yogurt mixture between 4 bowls and top each with a small handful of granola. Drizzle over some of the physalis coulis, then top with some berries and amaranth pop.

Avena de Quinua, Arándanos y Pecanas

SERVES 2

Quinoa, Cranberries & Pecan Porridge. *Porridge is comforting and warming, which is why the people of the Andes love it. It is also simple and packed with nutritious ingredients. If you don't fancy using cranberries and pecans, you can try cocoa and raisins, mango, or any fresh fruit that's in season.*

75g amaranth

100g white quinoa, cooked (see p.64)

40g cañigua or chia seeds

500ml almond milk

60g yacon syrup or honey

To serve

100g dried cranberries, or 100g of your favourite dried fruits or fresh berries

100g pecans, crumbled

A pinch of ground cinnamon

1–2 tbsp yacon syrup or honey

Rinse the amaranth, put it in a saucepan and cover with 150ml of water. Bring the water to the boil, then turn down the heat to low, cover the pan, and simmer the amaranth for 15 minutes until all the water has been absorbed. Remove the amaranth from the heat and allow to stand, covered, for a further 5 minutes. (You can do this while you're cooking the quinoa, if you like.)

Put the cooked quinoa, the cooked amaranth and the cañigua or chia seeds in a saucepan, cover with the almond milk and drizzle in the yacon syrup or honey, then stir to combine. Bring to the boil over a high heat, then turn down to a medium heat. Stir continuously for 15–20 minutes until the mixture has thickened to a rich and creamy porridge.

Serve the porridge in bowls with your chosen fruit and some crumbled pecans. Dust with a pinch of cinnamon and drizzle over more yacon syrup or honey.

Yawar Picante

SERVES 4

Black Pudding & Quail Eggs. *This recipe is based on one that my great aunts Carmela and Otilia used to make with chicken blood. I've suggested black pudding as an alternative, or you could use minced beef, if you prefer. My aunts often hosted morning gatherings and they would make this particular breakfast feast when they needed a favour from a neighbour! It's great for kids, too, as it contains tons of iron.*

60ml olive oil

2 large potatoes, peeled and cut into 1cm cubes

1 red onion, finely chopped

2 garlic cloves, crushed

4 medium-heat red chillies, deseeded and finely chopped, plus extra to serve

500ml beef or chicken blood, or 300g morcilla or black pudding

1 tsp smoked paprika

100ml dry cider

A few coriander leaves, finely chopped, plus extra to serve

A few mint leaves, finely chopped, plus extra to serve

Juice of 1 lime

12 quail eggs, medium–hard boiled, peeled and halved, to serve

2 spring onions, finely sliced, to serve

Salt and freshly ground black pepper

Heat the olive oil over a medium heat in a large, deep-sided frying pan or casserole. Add the potato and sauté for about 10 minutes, turning until all sides are lightly golden and crisp. Add the onion and continue to cook until the onion is lightly coloured and softened (about 10 minutes), then add the garlic and chilli. Cook for 2–3 minutes more, until the garlic has softened but hasn't taken on any colour.

Add the blood, morcilla or black pudding to the pan and sprinkle over the smoked paprika. Pour in the cider, season with salt and pepper, then sprinkle over the herbs. Cook gently for 10 minutes, stirring regularly, until any liquid has evaporated. Taste to check the seasoning, then pour in the lime juice and stir.

Pile the mixture onto a serving plate and serve scattered with the quail eggs, the chopped spring onions and extra chopped chilli and herbs.

Chicharrón con Huevo

SERVES 4

Confit Pork & Fried Egg. *A streetfood favourite, this is the dish that no Andina breakfast is complete without. Just south of the city of Cusco is the town of Saylla. There, you can find the best chicharrón in the Andes, but we think our version is even better. Usually, the sweet potato is deep fried, but for this recipe we have turned it into a smooth ketchup, making it creamy and less oily.*

600g pork belly, skin on, bone removed

Salt, for curing

2 dried bay leaves

1 tsp black peppercorns

1 sweet potato

Vegetable oil, for deep frying

4 brioche buns or crusty rolls, to serve

4 fried eggs, to serve

1 quantity of salsa criolla (see p.120), to serve

Salt and freshly ground black pepper

For the amarillo chilli mayonnaise

3 tbsp mayonnaise

1 tbsp amarillo chilli paste (see p.20)

¼ tsp dried oregano

¼ tsp garlic powder or ¼ mashed garlic clove

¼ tsp ground cumin

Cover the pork belly with salt on all sides, pressing in the salt as much as possible. Put the meat on a plate, cover it with a piece of kitchen paper and allow to cure in the fridge overnight.

When you are ready to cook, preheat the oven to 200°C (gas mark 6). Remove the pork from the fridge and rinse it thoroughly under running water to get rid of any excess salt. Put the meat in a roasting tin with the bay leaves and peppercorns. Cover with water, making sure the pork is completely submerged, including the skin. Cover the whole tin with foil and put it in the oven. Cook the meat for 1½–2 hours until tender. Prick the sweet potato all over and put it in a separate roasting tin and, about 1 hour into the pork's cooking time, place it in the oven on a different shelf and bake until the potato has softened (about 45 minutes).

Meanwhile, make the amarillo chilli mayonnaise. Mix together all the ingredients, then season with salt and pepper and set aside.

When ready, remove the sweet potato from the oven. As soon as it is cool enough to handle, peel away the skin and put the flesh in a food processor or blender. Purée with a little salt to taste, then allow to cool to room temperature, but do not chill.

When the pork is ready, remove it from the oven and allow to cool completely, then cut it into 3cm strips. Half-fill a large saucepan with vegetable oil, or use a deep-fat fryer, and heat until the oil until about 180°C. Add the chunks of pork to the oil and deep fry for 4–5 minutes until the skin is well browned and crisp. Remove the strips from the pan with a slotted spoon and set aside to drain on kitchen paper. Season with salt.

To serve, warm the buns or rolls, then cut in half. Spread a layer of sweet potato purée on one cut side of each of the buns or rolls, then spread the mayonnaise on the other cut side. Divide the pork equally between the bases, top each with a fried egg and some salsa criolla, season with salt to taste, then top with the bun lids.

Fuerza

SERVES 2

Breakfast in a Cup. Fuerza, *meaning 'strength', is warming, filling, quick to make and a meal in itself. It's like a strengthening breakfast in a cup. This recipe is a take on the hot quinoa drinks made by the Andina ladies who have street carts, and who get up at the crack of dawn to serve their own versions to their customers, adding unique combinations of herbs, spices and fruits.*

20g uncooked mixed quinoa (red, white and black), or 60g cooked mixed quinoa

500ml almond milk, plus extra to thin, if necessary

1 apple, cored and roughly chopped

1 tsp maca powder

If you're using uncooked quinoa, cook it according to the instructions on page 64.

Put the almond milk in a saucepan over a high heat. Add the cooked quinoa and the chopped apple. Bring to the boil, then reduce the heat to low and allow to simmer for 5 minutes until the apple is tender. Whisk in the maca powder.

Tip the contents of the saucepan into a food processor or blender and blitz until completely smooth. Serve hot (reheat it gently in a pan, if necessary). You can reheat any leftovers the following day.

Note: The result can be as liquid or as thick as you like – depending upon your preference and whether you want to drink it or to eat it with a spoon. Simply add more almond milk for a thinner consistency.

Panqueques de Camote

MAKES ABOUT 20 PANCAKES (SERVES 4–6)

Sweet Potato Pancakes. *Sweet potatoes are a great source of vitamins A and C, dietary fibre and a whole variety of minerals. A cheeky favourite at Andina, this recipe can have any kind of topping, but we think the mixture of fruit and whipped coconut cream is divine.*

175g plain flour

2 tsp baking powder

25g caster sugar

1 egg, plus 2 egg whites

225ml hazelnut milk

1 tsp vanilla extract

75g sweet potato purée (about 1 very small sweet potato; see p.30)

1 tbsp butter, melted, for frying

Chancaca syrup (see p.120) or yacon syrup, to serve

A few seasonal berries and a few physalis, to serve

For the coconut whipped cream

200ml whipping cream

50ml coconut cream

Put the plain flour, baking powder and caster sugar in a large bowl and stir to combine. Make a well in the centre and add the whole egg. Use a fork to whisk in the egg, incorporating flour from the sides of your well until you have a thick, almost unworkable paste. Gradually add the hazelnut milk, vanilla extract and sweet potato purée, whisking between each addition, until fully combined.

Whisk the egg whites to stiff peaks. Add 1 heaped tablespoon of the whisked egg white to the batter and stir in, then add the remaining egg white, stirring gently but thoroughly, keeping the mixture well aerated, until completely combined.

Brush a wide, shallow frying pan (or ideally a large pancake pan) with melted butter and set it over a medium–high heat. Add 3 or 4 generous tablespoons of the batter to the pan to create 3 or 4 individual pancakes. Allow the underside of each pancake to cook – you will see it set around the edges and large bubbles will appear on the surface of the pancake – then flip and cook the other side (about 3–4 minutes altogether). Set aside and repeat until you have used up all the batter.

To make the whipped coconut cream, put the ingredients in a bowl and use a hand-held electric whisk until it forms soft peaks.

To serve, arrange the pancakes on individual serving plates and top each with chancaca or yacon syrup and whipped coconut cream. Scatter with a few berries and halved physalis and serve immediately.

Piqueos

SNACKS

Berenjenas Fritas

SERVES 8

Aubergine Fries. *Aubergine is like the steak of the vegetable family: it is meaty, complex and juicy, and when it's cooked perfectly, there are few foods more delicious. These aubergine fries are light and make perfect partners for the sweet syrup and the yogurt dips.*

4 aubergines, peeled and cut into thick chips

50g cornmeal or polenta

50g chickpea flour

Vegetable oil, for deep frying

Salt and freshly ground black pepper

For the marinade

Crushed cloves of 1 garlic bulb

1 tsp dried oregano

75g amarillo chilli paste (see p.20)

50ml olive oil

For the chancaca & pomegranate syrup

150ml pomegranate juice

75g panela, palm sugar, jaggery or light soft brown sugar

½ limo chilli or 1 medium-heat red chilli, deseeded and finely chopped

For the yogurt dip

100g Greek yogurt

½ tsp muña powder or dried mint

A few fresh mint leaves or huacatay, chopped

A few pomegranate seeds, to serve

First, marinate the aubergine chips. Mix the marinade ingredients together with 1 teaspoon of salt. Add the aubergine chips and fold over gently until the chips are fully coated. Cover and marinate in the fridge overnight.

When you're ready to cook, first make the chancaca and pomegranate syrup. Put the juice, sugar and chilli into a small saucepan over a low heat. Simmer very gently, stirring regularly, until the sugar has completely dissolved, then reduce until the texture becomes syrupy (about 7–8 minutes). Transfer to a dipping bowl and set aside.

Next, make the yogurt dip. Mix the yogurt and muña powder or dried mint and the fresh mint or huacatay together and season with salt and pepper. Transfer to a dipping bowl, sprinkle with pomegranate seeds, then set aside.

Remove the aubergines from the marinade and pat dry if they have given out their liquid. Mix the cornmeal or polenta and chickpea flour together and season with salt. Dust the aubergine chips in the flour mixture.

Half-fill a large saucepan with vegetable oil, or use a deep-fat fryer, and heat the oil to about 180°C. Fry the aubergine chips in the oil for 3–4 minutes until they rise to the top and are crisp and golden brown. Remove the chips from the pan with a slotted spoon and set aside to drain on kitchen paper.

Serve the aubergine chips with pomegranate syrup and the yogurt dip on the side. To eat, dip the fries first in the syrup, then in the yogurt (hoping to pick up a pomegranate seed, too). The flavours will combine for a spectacular taste sensation!

Bombas de Ají Amarillo

SERVES 6

Amarillo Chilli Bombs. *At Casita Andina we call this the Russian roulette nibble – somewhere in the mix there is always a super-hot chilli, full of fire. Dare anyone to try. The combination of the crunchy amarillo chilli and the creamy mixture inside is perfect. For a vegetarian version, you can replace the bacon with the same amount of finely chopped asparagus.*

12 amarillo chillies or medium-heat red chillies

Micro herbs, such as marigold or coriander cress, or chopped chives or parsley, to serve

Salt

For the filling

50g butter

½ small red onion, finely chopped

25g button mushrooms, very finely chopped

1 tsp amarillo chilli paste (see p.20)

50g plain or gluten-free flour, plus extra for dusting

400ml full-fat milk

10g vegetarian Parmesan-like hard cheese, grated

15g feta, crumbled

1 tbsp olive oil

50g unsmoked back bacon, finely chopped

For the tempura batter

75g cornflour

50g gluten-free flour

1 tsp baking powder

100ml carbonated water

1 egg white, lightly beaten

First, make the filling. Heat the butter in a small saucepan over a low heat and add the onion and mushrooms. Sauté for about 10 minutes until the onion is soft and translucent, then add the chilli paste. Stir to combine, then sprinkle over the flour. Cook, stirring, over a low heat for 2–3 minutes until the butter and flour are combined and the flour has cooked out. Then, gradually add the milk, stirring continuously, until you have a thick béchamel. Stir in the cheeses. Keep stirring until they have melted, then remove from the heat. Blitz with a stick blender until smooth.

Heat the olive oil in a small frying pan over a medium heat and fry the bacon until crisp and brown. Stir this into the béchamel.

Prepare the chillies. Cut around the stem at the top of each chilli, then remove the insides: cut through the membranes, then insert a teaspoon and scrape along the inside of the flesh to scrape out the seeds. Take care not to tear the chillies.

Pour the béchamel mixture into a piping bag and pipe it into each chilli, or simply spoon teaspoonfuls of the mixture into each chilli, making sure it reaches all the way to the bottom. Each chilli should hold 35–40g of the mixture. Cut the filled chillies into bite-sized (about 4cm thick) slices, if necessary, and set aside.

Make the tempura batter by whisking all the ingredients together until smooth, then season with salt.

Dust the stuffed chillies with a little flour – this will help the batter stick to them – then dip each chilli in the batter. Half-fill a large saucepan with vegetable oil, or use a deep-fat fryer, and heat the oil to about 180°C. Carefully lower the chillies into the hot oil and fry until crisp and golden brown (about 4–5 minutes). Remove the chillies from the pan and set aside to drain on kitchen paper, then transfer to a serving platter, sprinkle with the herbs and serve immediately.

Ocopa Arequipeña con Raíces

SERVES 8

Arequipa Dip & Roots. *Doña Gladys, from the picantería La Lucila in Arequipa, patiently and slowly made the dip for this dish for me using a traditional batán millstone – a kind of large pestle and mortar. Here, we quicken things up with a food processor. If you can't get hold of oca tubers (native to the Andes, for an authentic touch), feel free to use any combination of root vegetable.*

1kg root vegetables – choose from parsnip, carrot, beetroot, celeriac, sweet potato and oca

3 tbsp olive oil

Salt and freshly ground black pepper

For the ocopa sauce

2 tbsp olive oil

1 red onion, finely chopped

4 confit garlic cloves (see p.76), crushed

6 amarillo chillies or medium-heat red chillies, deseeded and roughly chopped

1 tbsp panca chilli paste (see p.20)

60g peanuts

500ml evaporated milk; or 250ml full-fat milk mixed with 250ml single cream

A bunch of huacatay, or a small bunch each of mint, coriander, tarragon and parsley, leaves picked

4 cream crackers

40g queso fresco or feta, crumbled

Preheat the oven to 220°C (gas mark 7).

Peel the vegetables, then cut them into thick chips or wedges. Put all the vegetables, except the oca (if using), in a large roasting tin and drizzle over the olive oil. Season with plenty of salt and pepper. Turn the vegetables over until they are completely coated in the oil, then roast in the oven for 45–50 minutes until the vegetables are tender and lightly charred around the edges. If you're using oca, boil this for 10 minutes until tender, then add to the other vegetables in the oven for the last 10 minutes of cooking.

Meanwhile, make the ocopa sauce. Heat the olive oil in a frying pan over a low heat. Add the onion and sauté for about 8 minutes until softened, then add the garlic, chilli and chilli paste and sauté for 2–3 minutes more until the confit garlic has given out its flavour but hasn't taken on any colour. Remove the pan from the heat and allow the mixture to cool. Put the mixture in a food processor or blender with the peanuts, milk, herbs, cream crackers, and cheese. Season with salt and pepper, then blend until smooth and creamy.

Serve the root vegetables piping hot with the sauce on the side.

Croquetas de Maca

MAKES 24 (SERVES 8)

Maca Croquettes. *A firm favourite with anyone who pulls up a bar chair at Andina, these croquetas are lovingly rolled in full view of our customers by Head Chef Luca Depalo. The avocado yogurt dip is smooth and cooling – you can use it as a dip for this and many other yummy snacks, too.*

1 tbsp olive oil

1 small onion, finely chopped

15g piece of ginger, peeled and grated

60g plain yogurt

1 egg

120g feta, crumbled

60g polenta flour

60g gluten-free flour

5g maca powder

1 tsp baking powder

1 tsp bicarbonate of soda

½ tsp ground cumin

Vegetable oil, for deep frying

Coriander or parsley leaves, to serve

Salt and freshly ground black pepper

For the avocado yogurt

100g plain yogurt

½ ripe avocado, peeled, destoned and flesh mashed

Juice of ½ lime

To make the croquetas, put the olive oil in a small saucepan and add the onion. Sauté quite briskly over a medium heat until softened and slightly caramelized (about 10 minutes), then add the ginger. Cook for a further 1 minute, then remove from the heat and allow to cool.

Put the yogurt and egg in a large bowl with the feta and whisk to combine, then add the cooled onion and ginger mixture. In a separate bowl, mix all the dry ingredients together and season with plenty of salt and pepper, then incorporate into the yogurt, egg, onion and ginger mixture.

Form the mixture into 24 balls of equal size, then chill in the fridge for at least 1 hour.

Meanwhile, make the avocado yogurt by blitzing the ingredients together in a food processor or blender until smooth. Season with salt and pepper.

When you're ready to cook the croquetas, remove them from the fridge. Half-fill a large saucepan with vegetable oil, or use a deep-fat fryer, and heat the oil to about 180°C. Fry the croquetas in batches, removing them with a slotted spoon when they float to the top and are a deep golden brown. Set aside to drain on kitchen paper, then transfer to a serving plate.

Serve sprinkled with a few coriander or parsley leaves and with the avocado yogurt on the side for dipping.

Vegetarian, Gluten-free

Torrejas de Sachaca

MAKES 8 LARGE OR 16 SMALL FRITTERS

Sachaca's Carrot Fritters. *Sachaca in Arequipa is a hotspot for the best carrot fritters in the Andes. Sisters Gladys and Ruth, from La Lucila in Sachaca, gave me some tips on how to make this quick and delicious recipe that's perfect for when you want to entertain friends, or if you just want to enjoy a crunchy vegetarian fritter as a snack. It's also a great dish for kids – beats any burger and chips.*

75g plain flour

125ml carbonated water

2 large carrots (about 250g), peeled and coarsely grated

1 white onion, finely chopped or grated

2 garlic cloves, crushed

A few parsley sprigs, finely chopped

Vegetable oil, for frying

Salt and freshly ground black pepper

For the rocoto llactan sauce (makes about 150ml)

1 rocoto pepper or 2 medium-heat red chillies, or (for extra heat) 1 Scotch bonnet

1 red onion, roughly chopped

A bunch of huacatay, or a small bunch each of coriander, parsley, mint and tarragon

2 tbsp cancha corn or raw peanuts, toasted

30g queso fresco or feta

A small bunch of wild garlic leaves, or ½ garlic clove

First, make the rocoto llactan sauce. Either pound everything together with a little water in a large mortar, or pulse very carefully in a food processor or blender – you are aiming for a fairly coarse texture. Season with salt and pepper.

To make the fritters, whisk the flour and water together until you have a thick batter. When you are ready to fry the fritters, stir in the remaining ingredients and season with salt and pepper. (Make sure you stir in the vegetables just before frying, or they will have time to release liquid into the batter.)

Cover the base of a large frying pan with a generous amount of vegetable oil and heat until the air above it is starting to shimmer. Drop large, heaped spoonfuls of the fritter batter into the hot oil and press down lightly. (Note: use a serving spoon for large fritters and a tablespoon for small.) Fry for 2–4 minutes on each side until crisp and brown. Remove from the pan with a slotted spoon and set aside to drain on kitchen paper. Repeat until you have used up all the batter.

Season the fritters with a little more salt and serve hot with the rocoto llactan sauce on the side.

Bolitas de Chancho con Rocoto

MAKES 24 (SERVES 8)

Pork Balls with Rocoto Jam. *I love these cheeky, fiery meatballs. They are perfect for kids, but also for grown-ups as a snack – with a beer. The rocoto jam has a nice kick to balance the sweetness. This version is pork-based, but the meatballs will also work well with leftover beef, chicken or fish.*

2 tbsp achiote oil (see p.146)

1 small red onion, finely chopped

2 garlic cloves, finely chopped

75g panca chilli paste (see p.20)

100g pig liver, very finely chopped

200g minced pork

80g plain flour, plus extra to coat the meatballs

1 tsp ground cumin

1 egg, lightly beaten

Vegetable oil, for deep frying

Salt and freshly ground black pepper

For the rocoto jam (makes about 100g)

2 rocoto peppers or medium-heat red chillies, deseeded and finely chopped

2 tbsp granulated sugar

Heat the achiote oil in a large pan over a medium heat. Add the onion, cook for about 10 minutes until softened, then add the garlic and the chilli paste. Cook for 3–4 minutes, then add the liver and pork and cook for 5 minutes more, stirring until everything is well combined. Sprinkle in the flour and cumin and cook over a low heat, stirring, until the flour has disappeared and the texture is thick. Remove the pan from the heat, allow to cool a little, then mix in the egg. Season, cool, then refrigerate to cool completely.

Meanwhile, make the rocoto jam. Put the rocoto pepper or chilli and the sugar in a small saucepan with 25ml of water. Stir over a low heat until the sugar has dissolved, then turn up the heat and reduce the mixture to the consistency of warm jam (about 10 minutes). Allow to cool. (Refrigerate any unused jam in a sterilized jar for up to 4 weeks.)

When you are ready to cook the pork balls, remove the pork mixture from the fridge and form it into 24 small balls (about 25g each). Roll them in flour and dust off any excess. Half-fill a large saucepan with vegetable oil, or use a deep-fat fryer, and heat the oil to about 180°C. Fry the bolitas in batches for about 5–6 minutes until they are crisp and golden brown. Remove from the pan with a slotted spoon and set aside to drain on kitchen paper, then transfer to a serving plate and serve with the jam alongside for dipping.

Tempura de Palta

SERVES 4

Avocado Tempura. *Crispy and thin on the outside and warm and creamy on the inside, this delicate and decadent nibble, created by our Executive Chef Vito, simply explodes with amazing flavour. Best of all, it's virtually effortless to make.*

Vegetable oil, for deep frying

3 ripe avocados, destoned, peeled and flesh cut into large cubes

Lime wedges, to serve

For the spice mix

20g dried anchovies
or smoked paprika

10g panca chilli powder, or chipotle or any smoked chilli powder

¼ tsp ground cumin

¼ tsp garlic powder

¼ tsp salt

For the tempura batter

100g gluten-free flour

1 tbsp gluten-free baking powder

75ml carbonated water

1 egg white, beaten

Salt

First, make the spice mix. If you are using dried anchovies, dry fry them over a low heat for about 20 minutes until they are very aromatic and crisp. Allow to cool, then put them in a food processor or spice grinder and blitz to a fine powder. Mix the anchovy powder or smoked paprika with the remaining spice mix ingredients until fully combined. Transfer to a clean, airtight jar to store (you need only a sprinkling for this recipe, so save the remainder for another day – it will keep for up to 4 weeks).

To make the tempura batter, put the flour and baking powder in a bowl, season with salt, then whisk everything together. Pour in the carbonated water and egg white and whisk again until the batter is smooth.

Half-fill a large saucepan with vegetable oil, or use a deep-fat fryer, and heat the oil to about 180°C. Dip the avocado cubes in the batter and immediately transfer to the oil (do this in 2–3 batches, if necessary). When the fritters are floating and have a crisp, golden exterior (about 3–4 minutes), remove them from the pan with a slotted spoon and set aside to drain on kitchen paper, before transferring them to a serving plate.

Serve the fritters with a squeeze of lime and a little sprinkling of the spice mix.

Papa a la Huancaína

SERVES 4

Potatoes with Huancayo Sauce. *You'll find this dish all over Peru, but some of the best versions come from the beautiful city of Huancayo. Famous for its potatoes, Huancayo also gives us the magnificent sauce that carries its name – Peruvians all over the world crave it.*

200g new potatoes, thickly sliced

200g purple heritage potatoes or sweet potatoes, thickly sliced

4 quail eggs

160g queso fresco or halloumi, cut into 4 triangular wedges

1 tbsp plain flour, for dusting

1 egg, beaten

60g panko breadcrumbs

Vegetable oil, for deep frying

8 Peruvian botija olives, or Kalamata olives, pitted and halved, to serve

1 tbsp pecans, chopped, to serve

Salt and freshly ground black pepper

For the Huancayo sauce

3 tbsp olive oil

1 onion, finely chopped

1 small garlic clove, finely chopped

½ amarillo chilli or medium-heat red chilli, deseeded and roughly chopped

30g queso fresco or feta

150ml evaporated milk

3 cream crackers, broken up

First, make the Huancayo sauce. Heat the olive oil in a frying pan over a low heat. Add the onion and sauté gently until very soft and translucent, then add the garlic and chilli and sauté for a further 2–3 minutes until the garlic has started to soften but hasn't taken on any colour. Remove from the heat and allow to cool slightly. Put the onion mixture in a food processor or blender with the remaining ingredients and blitz until smooth, then decant to a jug or bowl and set aside.

Put the potato slices in a saucepan and cover with water. Salt the water, then turn up the heat to high and bring to the boil. Lower the heat and simmer for about 10 minutes until the potato slices are just tender. Set aside and allow to cool until close to room temperature.

Bring a small saucepan of water to the boil. Add the quail eggs and boil fiercely for 3 minutes. Remove the eggs using a slotted spoon and immediately plunge into iced water to stop them cooking. Peel and cut the eggs in half lengthways.

Dust the queso fresco or halloumi wedges in the flour, patting off any excess, then dip each one in the beaten egg and coat in the breadcrumbs. Half-fill a large saucepan with vegetable oil, or use a deep-fat fryer, and heat the oil to about 180°C. Fry the cheese triangles until the breadcrumbs are golden brown (about 3–4 minutes). Remove the cheese from the pan with a slotted spoon and set aside to drain well on kitchen paper.

To assemble the dish, divide the potatoes equally between 4 plates and drizzle over the Huancayo sauce. Add a slice of cheese to each plate along with 2 quail egg halves. Sprinkle over the olive halves and pecans and serve immediately.

Ensaladas

SALADS

Sandía, Quinua Negra y Queso Fresco

SERVES 4

Infused Watermelon & Fresco Cheese Salad. *The intense flavour of infused watermelon in this dish blends perfectly with nutty black quinoa and creamy, sour queso fresco. Use feta cheese if you can't find queso fresco; and although the black quinoa gives this dish a nutty twist, white quinoa would do nicely, too.*

30g yacon syrup or
50g granulated sugar

2 limo chillies or medium-heat red chillies, finely chopped

240g watermelon, cut into
4 large pieces

40g uncooked black quinoa

100g queso fresco or feta, crumbled, to serve

30g watercress leaves, to serve

For the lemon & almond vinaigrette

Pared zest of 1 lemon

40g whole almonds, toasted and roughly crushed

50ml olive oil

10ml Moscatel vinegar, or white wine vinegar mixed with a pinch of sugar

Salt

Make a simple syrup by putting the yacon syrup or sugar in a small saucepan with 50ml of water. Simmer over a low heat, stirring continuously until the sugar (if using) has dissolved and the mixture has fully combined. Then, add the chilli and watermelon pieces. Transfer everything to a plastic self-seal bag or a storage container and allow to infuse.

Meanwhile, make the vinaigrette. Put the lemon zest in a small saucepan and cover with water. Bring to the boil over a high heat and add a pinch of salt. Reduce the heat to low and simmer for 5 minutes to help remove any bitterness. Drain the zest and set under running cold water until cool, then repeat the procedure, boiling, simmering and draining again. When the zest has cooled for the second time, slice it very finely, then put it in a small bowl and mix in the remaining ingredients. Set aside.

Cook the quinoa according to the instructions on page 64 and allow to cool.

To assemble the dish, place 1 piece of watermelon on each of 4 plates. Sprinkle a quarter of the quinoa over each serving, then do the same with the feta and watercress. Drizzle over the dressing and serve immediately.

Arrollado de Palta

SERVES 4

Avocado & Jerusalem Artichoke Roll. *At our restaurants we put great effort into creating the tastiest, healthiest and prettiest salads we can. This is a prime example. The creamy avocado, ripe and tender Jerusalem artichoke and the amarillo chilli tiger's milk make for a delicious, nutritious and gorgeous starter or side dish.*

2 ripe avocados

A few black amaranth micro herbs or purple shiso leaves

2 tbsp cooked black quinoa (see p.64), to serve

1 tbsp coriander herb oil (see below), to serve

Avocado purée, to serve (optional; see p.58)

A few coriander micro herbs, to decorate

For the Jerusalem artichoke tartare

2 large Jerusalem artichokes (about 100–120g), peeled and diced

½ limo chilli or medium-heat red chilli, deseeded and finely chopped

½ small red onion, finely chopped

A few coriander leaves, finely chopped

4 tbsp amarillo tiger's milk (see p.74)

Salt

For the coriander herb oil

5 coriander sprigs

5 tbsp olive oil

First, make the Jerusalem artichoke tartare. Bring a saucepan of salted water to the boil. Add the diced artichoke and blanch for 4 minutes – it should still have some bite to it. Drain the artichoke pieces, cool them under running water, then put them in a small bowl with the chilli, red onion, coriander leaves and 2 tablespoons of the amarillo tiger's milk. Season with salt, then marinate in the fridge for at least 1 hour.

Meanwhile, make the coriander herb oil by blitzing the ingredients together with a stick blender. Set aside. (You can store any unused herb oil in a sterilized jar for up to 4 weeks.)

Divide the tartare between 4 plates, arranging it in a sausage shape. Halve the avocados, remove the stones and peel, then thinly slice the flesh. Divide the avocado slices between the 4 plates, draping them over the tartare, then top with the amaranth micro herbs or shiso leaves and a little quinoa.

Drizzle equal amounts of the remaining amarillo tiger's milk over each plate, then the coriander oil and a little avocado purée (if using), and finally decorate with the coriander micro herbs and serve immediately.

Vegetarian, Vegan, Gluten-free

Causa Puno

SERVES 4

Purple Potato, Tuna & Rocoto Pepper Causa. *Causas are cold mashed-potato salads, topped usually with avocado and other ingredients. We love making them, and this one has been a real favourite as a result of its balance of textures, colours and flavours. You can use cooked octopus or any other fresh fish instead of tuna, if you prefer.*

200g purple potatoes or regular floury potatoes

3 tbsp amarillo chilli paste (see p.20)

1 tbsp lime juice

2 tbsp olive oil

A few purple shiso leaves or small basil leaves, to decorate

Salt and freshly ground black pepper

For the tuna tartare

50ml rocoto tiger's milk (see p.82), plus extra (optional) for drizzling

1 tbsp mayonnaise

150g tuna fillet, chilled and finely chopped

For the avocado purée

1 large ripe avocado

A squeeze of lime juice

First, cook the potatoes. Leave them in their skins, put them in a large saucepan and cover them with water. Put the pan over a high heat and bring to the boil, then cook the potatoes until just tender (about 15–20 minutes). Remove the pan from the heat and drain. When they are cool enough to handle, peel them and mash the flesh. Add the chilli paste to the mash, along with the lime juice and olive oil and season well with salt and pepper. Allow to cool.

To make the tuna tartare, whisk together the rocoto tiger's milk and the mayonnaise, then season with salt and pepper. Add the tuna and stir to combine, then cover and leave the tartare to chill in the fridge until you are ready to serve.

To make the avocado purée, halve the avocado, remove the stone and peel the halves. Put the avocado flesh with the squeeze of lime juice and a pinch of salt in a food processor or blender and blitz until smooth.

To assemble the dish, divide the potato mixture into 4 equal portions and shape each into a round patty, like a burger. Place one patty on each of 4 plates. Spoon a quarter of the avocado purée on top of each patty, then top with equal portions of the tuna tartare and drizzle with a little more rocoto tiger's milk, if you wish. Decorate with the shiso leaves and serve immediately.

Ensalada Chullo

SERVES 4

Roasted Pumpkin, Beetroot & Orange. *Colourful, refreshing and elegant, this salad makes for a perfect starter. It's great for using up leftover Halloween pumpkin, but you can also use squash, which is more readily available all year round. If you can't find physalis coulis (or jam; you'll need this to make the dressing) or you haven't got time to make it yourself, use orange or any citrus-based marmalade.*

250g pumpkin, peeled, deseeded and cut into 1cm slices

½ tbsp cloves

1 tbsp dried thyme

2 tbsp olive oil

250g cooked beetroot, sliced

1 orange, segmented, to serve

2 large handfuls of baby salad leaves, to serve

A few popcorn shoots or 2 spring onions, finely chopped, to serve

Salt and freshly ground black pepper

For the mustard beetroot

75g cooked beetroot

2 tbsp olive oil

½ tsp mustard powder

1 tsp sherry vinegar

For the physalis dressing

1 tbsp physalis coulis (see p.26)

3 tbsp olive oil

15ml Moscatel vinegar, or white wine vinegar and a pinch of sugar

1 tsp amarillo chilli paste (see p.20)

Preheat the oven to 180°C (gas mark 4).

Put the pumpkin in a roasting tin and sprinkle over the cloves and dried thyme. Drizzle over the olive oil and toss everything together to coat in the oil, then season with salt and pepper. Roast in the oven for 30 minutes until the pumpkin is cooked through and lightly charred. Remove from the oven and allow to cool.

Meanwhile, make the mustard beetroot. Put the beetroot in a food processor or blender with the olive oil, mustard powder and sherry vinegar. Season with salt and pepper and blitz until smooth, then set aside.

For the physalis dressing, whisk the coulis with the olive oil, vinegar and chilli paste, then season with salt and pepper and set aside.

To assemble the salad, divide the beetroot slices and roasted pumpkin between 4 plates. Add spoonfuls of the mustard beetroot and drizzle with the physalis dressing. Decorate with the orange segments, baby salad leaves and the popcorn shoots or spring onions and serve immediately.

Sarza de Patitas

SERVES 2

Marinated Pigs' Trotters. *This cold, refreshing and meaty salad is one of the Arequipa region's most emblematic dishes. It's also very economical. Nose-to-tail eating is ingrained in our Andina culture and ensures greater sustainability: we use as much of the animal as possible to create nutritious dishes and generate less waste.*

4 small pigs' trotters

1 carrot, julienned

3 celery sticks, roughly chopped

1 large red onion, roughly chopped

4 garlic cloves, bruised

3 dried bay leaves

½ tsp peppercorns

2 red onions, finely sliced

2 tomatoes, halved and finely sliced

A small bunch of parsley, finely chopped, to serve

2 large potatoes, cooked and sliced, to serve

Salt

For the marinade

4 tbsp olive oil

2 tbsp red wine vinegar

Juice of 3 limes

2 dried bay leaves, crumbled

1 tsp dried oregano

1 garlic clove, crushed

1 rocoto pepper or 2 medium-heat red chillies, deseeded and finely chopped

Put the pigs' trotters in a large saucepan and cover with water. Put the pan over a high heat and bring the water to the boil. Immediately, mushroom-coloured foam will collect on the surface of the water – skim this away. When the foam stops forming, add the carrot, celery, roughly chopped red onion and the garlic, along with the bay leaves, 2 teaspoons of salt and the peppercorns. Turn down the heat to low and simmer for 1½–2 hours until the trotter meat is tender and on the verge of falling off the bone. Remove the trotters carefully with a slotted spoon and transfer to a bowl to cool.

While the trotters are cooling, mix together all the marinade ingredients and season with salt. When the trotters have cooled, add the sliced onion to the bowl and pour over the marinade, turning everything gently to coat. Cover the bowl with clingfilm and leave to marinate in the fridge overnight.

To assemble the dish, place the trotters on 2 individual serving plates, reserving the marinade. Add half the slices of red onion (from the marinade liquid) and half the slices of tomatoes to each plate, then spoon over the reserved marinade liquid, season with salt and finish off with a sprinkle of chopped parsley. Serve the potatoes on the side.

Causa de Alcachofa de Jerusalén

SERVES 4

Sweet Potato & Jerusalem Artichoke Causa. *Causa, meaning 'cause', is a Peruvian dish with a story. During Peru's last major war, food was running low; only potatoes and scraps were left. The wives of the soldiers on the front line created a dish to make the most of the potato, adding remaining ingredients as toppings. When they handed the food to their husbands, they said 'This is for the cause.'*

400g floury potatoes, skin on, left whole

2 tbsp olive oil

3 tbsp amarillo chilli paste (see p.20)

2 tbsp rocoto pepper paste (see below)

1 quantity of Jerusalem artichoke tartare (see p.56)

1 quantity of avocado purée (see p.58)

A few edible flowers, such as violas, to decorate (optional)

Salt

For the rocoto pepper paste

1 tbsp olive oil

¼ onion, finely chopped

1 rocoto pepper, or 1 medium-heat red chilli and 1 habanero or Scotch bonnet, deseeded and finely chopped

2 garlic cloves, crushed

For the sweet potato purée

½ small sweet potato, skin on

For the artichoke crisps

1 artichoke, peeled and very finely sliced

Vegetable oil, for deep frying

First, make the rocoto pepper paste. Heat the oil in a small frying pan over a medium heat. Add the onion and sauté for 8–10 minutes until soft, then add the pepper or chillies and the garlic and sauté for 2–3 minutes more to soften. Allow to cool, then use a mini-processor or stick blender to blitz to a paste. Store until needed.

Put the potatoes in a saucepan and cover with water. Salt the water, then bring to the boil over a high heat and cook for 15–20 minutes until the potatoes are tender. Drain the potatoes. As soon as they are cool enough to handle, peel them and tip them back in the pan. Mash thoroughly, then stir through the olive oil and chilli and pepper pastes. Season with salt. Allow to cool to room temperature.

To make the sweet potato purée, bring a small saucepan of water to the boil over a high heat and add the sweet potato half. Reduce the heat to low and simmer for 10 minutes until the sweet potato is tender, then remove the pan from the heat and drain. As soon as it is cool enough to handle, peel the potato and tip it back in the dry pan, then season with salt and mash to a smooth purée.

To make the artichoke crisps, blot the artichoke slices with kitchen paper and sprinkle with salt – this gets them as dry as possible. Half-fill a small saucepan with vegetable oil and heat it to about 180°C. Drop in the artichoke slices and fry until very crisp and curled up (about 3–4 minutes). Remove with a slotted spoon and set aside to drain on kitchen paper.

To assemble the salad, form the potato mixture into 16–20 small rolls and divide between 4 plates. Arrange the artichoke tartare on top of the potato rolls, then add equal amounts of the sweet potato and avocado purées and the artichoke crisps to the plates. Decorate with edible flowers, if using, and serve immediately.

Ensalada Sierra

SERVES 4

Quinoa & Avocado Salad. *The combination of the crunch of the quinoa, fresh ingredients such as cucumber, tomato and radish, and a sharp tiger's milk with a sweet chilli dressing, gives this dish great depth of flavour that provides a wonderful culinary journey for your palate.*

100g uncooked mixed quinoa
(red, black and white)

100g cooked butter beans

½ medium-heat red chilli,
deseeded and finely sliced

1 red onion, diced

2 tbsp amarillo tiger's milk
(see p.74)

2 tbsp olive oil

1 ripe avocado

8 cherry tomatoes, halved

2 radishes, finely sliced

1 cucumber, cut into 4 chunks, then
into cylinders using an apple corer

A handful of physalis, halved

1 tbsp pomegranate seeds

2 tbsp rocoto jam (see p.48)

2 tbsp uchucuta sauce (see p.132)

Salt

First, cook the quinoa. Put the quinoa in a saucepan over a medium heat. Cover with 200ml of water and season with salt. Bring the water to the boil, then turn down the heat to a gentle simmer and cover. Cook for 15 minutes, then remove from the heat and allow to stand, covered, for a further 5 minutes. The quinoa should have absorbed all the water, the tail should have unfurled and the grains should be tender (check the red and black quinoa, as they can take a little longer than the white to become tender). Allow to cool.

When you are ready to assemble the salad, put the quinoa in a bowl with the butter beans, chilli and red onion. Stir gently to combine, then drizzle over the amarillo tiger's milk and the olive oil.

To serve, halve and destone the avocado, then roughly mash the flesh with a fork. Divide the mash equally between 4 plates and top with equal amounts of the quinoa mixture. Then to each plate add tomatoes, radish slices, cucumber cylinders, physalis halves and a sprinkling of pomegranate seeds. Thin down the rocoto jam with a little water to make a pourable sauce, then drizzle over a little of this and a little uchucuta sauce to finish off each salad plate. Serve immediately.

Vegetarian, Gluten-free

Solterito

SERVES 4

Broad Bean, Tomato, Fresco Cheese & Botija Olive Salad. *The word* solterito *means 'unmarried' and I find it intriguing that this emblematic Arequipa dish gets its name because it was once eaten only by unmarried men. Light but filling, the salad helped loveless bachelors to stay svelte while each one searched for a wife. I love this as a main at lunchtime: it bursts with flavour and is bright to look at.*

125g purple potatoes or regular floury potatoes

125g new potatoes

75g broad beans

75g choclo corn kernels or sweetcorn kernels

8 cherry tomatoes, halved

8 Peruvian botija olives, or Kalamata olives, halved

1 amarillo chilli or medium-heat red chilli, deseeded and julienned

75g queso fresco, crumbled, or 75g cottage cheese

2 spring onions, very thinly sliced, to serve

Salt and freshly ground black pepper

For the dressing

75ml olive oil

50ml white wine vinegar

½ tbsp rocoto pepper paste (see p.62)

A few parsley leaves, finely torn

¼ small red onion, finely chopped

Put all the potatoes in a saucepan and cover with water. Put over a high heat and bring to the boil. Salt the water and cook the potatoes until tender (about 15 minutes), then drain and allow to cool. Cut into cubes or thick slices.

Bring another saucepan of water to the boil over a high heat. Salt the water, then add the broad beans and choclo or sweetcorn and cook for 3–4 minutes until just tender. Drain and allow to cool.

Meanwhile, make the dressing. Whisk the olive oil and white wine vinegar together with the rocoto paste and season with salt and pepper. Stir through the parsley leaves and red onion, then set aside. (Store any leftover dressing in a sterilized jar in the fridge for up to 2 weeks.)

To assemble the salad, put the potatoes, broad beans and choclo or sweetcorn in a bowl with the cherry tomatoes, olives and julienned chilli. Add the cheese, pour in the dressing and stir to combine. Finally, decorate with a sprinkling of spring onions.

Vegetarian, Gluten-free

Sarza de Criadillas

SERVES 4–6

Testes, Baby Sweetcorn & Broad Bean Sarza. *In the Andes this dish is loved and enjoyed as much today as it was thousands of years ago. My focus is always on delicious flavours and this salad offers just that. The meat is tender and therefore absorbs the sharp, scrumptious seasoning. With the crunchy vegetables, too, it makes for a unique salad.*

600g cow's or sheep's testicles
(about 6 testicles)

200g broad beans, blanched
and peeled

2 potatoes, boiled until tender,
cooled and sliced

8 uncooked baby sweetcorn, sliced
in half lengthways

½ red pepper, deseeded and cut
into strips

½ green pepper, deseeded and cut
into strips

½ yellow pepper, deseeded and cut
into strips

1 red onion, sliced

Salt and freshly ground black pepper

For the marinade

1 garlic clove, crushed

1 rocoto pepper or 2 medium-heat
red chillies, deseeded and finely
chopped

1 tomato, finely diced

2 dried bay leaves

A few parsley leaves, finely
chopped, plus extra to decorate

60ml olive oil

90ml white wine vinegar

First, prepare the testicles. Boil them in a pan of water for 5 minutes. Leave the water boiling, but remove the testicles with a slotted spoon and refresh them in a bowl of iced water. Then, put them back in the pan and boil again for 10 minutes, then drain. As soon as the testicles are cool enough to handle, pull the membrane layers away from the flesh, taking care that none of the flesh comes away, too. The membrane should come off in one piece, leaving you with a large egg-shaped testicle that is very soft and the colour of chicken breast.

Put the testicles in cold, salted water and leave for about 6 hours, changing the water every 2 hours or so.

When you are ready to cook the testicles, bring a large saucepan of well-salted water to the boil over a high heat. Drop in the testicles. Turn down the heat to low and poach the testicles gently for about 30 minutes – when they are done, they will have very little give and will have shrunk considerably. Drain and cool in iced water, then cut each testicle into 6 wedges or slices and pull out any obvious veins.

Mix all the marinade ingredients together in a bowl and add the cooled testicle pieces. Season with salt and pepper, then cover and refrigerate overnight.

To assemble the salad, remove the bay leaves from the bowl, then add the remaining ingredients and stir to combine. Sprinkle over a few chopped parsley leaves to decorate and serve immediately.

Ceviches

CEVICHES

Ceviche Andino

SERVES 4

Sea Bass, Physalis & Avocado Ceviche. *This is one of our most iconic dishes at Andina. Although associated with the coast, in fact ceviches are eaten all over Peru, especially in the Andes where there is a wide variety of river fish. In this recipe, we have brought together some key Andina ingredients to create a ceviche that sings with authenticity.*

1 large red onion, very thinly sliced

1 sweet potato, peeled and cut into 1.5cm dice

600g skinless sea bass fillets, cut into 1.5cm dice

A few coriander leaves, finely chopped; plus a few extra whole leaves, to decorate

1 large, ripe avocado, destoned, peeled and flesh cut into 1.5cm dice

12 physalis, halved

2 tsp cancha corn or pistachios, crushed, to serve

4 tbsp coriander herb oil (see p.56)

Salt

For the amarillo tiger's milk (makes about 200ml)

5mm piece of ginger

1 garlic clove, halved

4 coriander sprigs

Juice of 12 limes, plus extra to taste

2 tsp amarillo chilli paste (see p.20)

First, make the amarillo tiger's milk. Put the ginger, garlic, coriander and lime juice in a bowl. Stir and leave to infuse for 10 minutes. Strain the mixture through a sieve into a separate bowl and add the chilli paste and ½ teaspoon of salt. Taste to check the balance of flavours and add more salt, chilli or lime juice if necessary. Set aside.

Meanwhile, soak the onion slices in iced water for 5 minutes, then drain them thoroughly and lay them out on kitchen paper so that they dry completely.

Bring a small saucepan of water to the boil. Salt the water then add the sweet potato cubes. Reduce the heat to low and simmer until just tender (about 5–7 minutes). Drain and set aside.

Put the cubes of sea bass in the bowl with the tiger's milk for 1 minute only, then add the onion slices, chopped coriander, avocado, physalis, and the cooked sweet potato. Turn all the components over very gently (you do not want the sweet potato or avocado to break up), then divide the ceviche equally between 4 bowls. Taste and check the seasoning, adding a little more salt if necessary, then serve immediately decorated with a sprinkling of crushed cancha corn or pistachios, coriander leaves and coriander herb oil.

Sivinche

SERVES 4

Pre-Inca Prawn Tartare. *Forget steak tartare, this dish has far more funk and punk, is deeper and more daring, and – to top it off – harbours thousands of years of history. River prawns are a speciality in the region of Arequipa, thanks to their exquisitely intense flavour, but you can use super-fresh sea prawns, if that's all that you have available.*

8 very large raw king prawns, peeled, heads removed, deveined and very finely chopped

1 red onion, finely chopped

2 tomatoes, deseeded and finely chopped

4 parsley sprigs, leaves picked and finely chopped

2 tarragon sprigs, leaves picked and finely chopped

2 mint sprigs, leaves picked and finely chopped

1 medium-heat red chilli, deseeded and finely chopped

Hot toast, buttered or drizzled with olive oil; or 200g new potatoes, steamed and sliced, to serve

1 ripe avocado, halved, destoned, peeled and flesh chopped (optional), to serve

Salt and freshly ground black pepper

For the dressing

4 confit garlic cloves (see note, right)

8 peppercorns

50ml chicha (see p.199) or dry cider

4 tbsp red wine vinegar

4 tbsp olive oil

Put the finely chopped king prawns in a bowl and season with salt. Add the red onion and tomato, the herbs and the chilli and stir to combine. Set aside.

Next, make the dressing. Put the confit garlic in a mortar with the peppercorns and a pinch of salt, then pound with the pestle until the pepper is crushed and the garlic is well mashed. Tip this mixture into a small bowl and add the remaining dressing ingredients. Stir together thoroughly, pour the dressing over the prawns and stir thoroughly again.

Allow to stand for 10 minutes, then serve as a tartare on toast or accompanied by new potatoes and a cheeky addition of slices of ripe avocado seasoned with salt and pepper (avocado and prawn makes a great partnership), if you wish.

Note: It's easy to make your own confit garlic cloves. Simply separate and peel the cloves from 2 heads of garlic and put them in a small saucepan with enough olive oil to cover. Put the pan over a medium heat and bring the oil just up to a simmer (but don't let it boil), then immediately reduce the heat to very low. Allow the cloves to poach in the oil for about 20 minutes, until very soft but holding together. Allow to cool, then transfer everything (including the oil) to a sterilized airtight jar and store for up to 6 weeks.

Ceviche de Tarwi

SERVES 4

Chermo's Bean Ceviche. *You would find this quick and simple dish as a nibble, side dish or starter in many restaurants in the region of La Libertad. It's also a favourite of my beloved godfather Chermo. A former policeman, he knows every great restaurant and picantería in the northern Andes of Peru, so in tribute to his talented palate, I dedicate this dish to him.*

500g cooked white beans, preferably lupin or large cannellini

1 red onion, finely sliced

1 rocoto pepper or 2 medium-heat red chillies, deseeded and finely chopped

1 large tomato, deseeded and diced

2 tbsp finely chopped coriander

1 tbsp finely chopped parsley

A few handfuls of cancha corn, to serve

For the dressing

4 tbsp olive oil

Juice of 3 lemons

Salt and freshly ground black pepper

Put the beans, onion, rocoto pepper or chilli and the tomato in a large bowl. Gently stir to combine, being careful not to break up any of the beans.

To make the dressing, whisk the olive oil with the lemon juice and season with salt and pepper.

Stir the dressing through the bean and herb mixture and serve in a bowl, with a bowl of cancha corn on the side.

Tiradito de Trucha

SERVES 4

Trout Tiradito. *In the Andes the cold, fast-flowing, crystal-clear rivers make for the most exquisite trout you'll ever find. Use the freshest, best-grade fish fillet you can buy – this is a light, delicate dish that relies on the quality of its ingredients. This tiradito is a show-stopper at Casita Andina: it's worth taking your time over the presentation.*

250g purple potatoes or regular floury potatoes, skin on, left whole

1 tsp amaranth

60g trout roe

400g skinless rainbow trout fillets, well chilled and finely sliced

1 quantity of amarillo tiger's milk (see p.74)

A few nasturtium, purple shiso, or watercress leaves, to serve

Coriander herb oil (see p.56) or a few coriander leaves, to serve

Hot paprika, to serve

Salt

Put the potatoes in a saucepan and cover with water. Bring to the boil and add a good pinch of salt. Boil the potatoes for about 15–20 minutes until tender. Drain, then as soon as the potatoes are cool enough to handle, peel them and mash until very smooth. Allow to cool completely, then divide up the mash into 4 equal portions. Shape the portions into evenly sized cylinders, then wrap each one in clingfilm. Chill in the fridge.

Heat a small frying pan over a medium heat and add the amaranth. Heat the amaranth until it starts to pop open, then remove from the pan quickly onto a side plate to stop it burning.

To serve, unwrap the potato cylinders and cut each one into 3 or 4 lengths. Arrange the potato pieces on individual serving plates and top each potato piece with a small amount of the trout roe. Arrange slices of trout fillet around the potato pieces and then flood each plate with the tiger's milk. Sprinkle over the toasted amaranth, the nasturtium or watercress leaves, coriander herb oil or leaves, and paprika, then serve immediately.

Yana Ceviche

SERVES 4

Tuna, Pickled Pineapple & Black Quinoa Ceviche. *This delicate and stylish ceviche has become a classic at Andina. It has the zesty and lightly fiery flavour of the rocoto tiger's milk, with the sharp flavour of the pineapple and the nuttiness and crunch of the black quinoa. It ends with the soft, creamy texture of the tuna.*

300g skinless tuna fillet, cut into 2cm cubes and chilled

A few samphire sprigs, blanched

15g black radish, very finely sliced

120g cooked black quinoa (see p.64), to serve

A few coriander cress or watercress leaves

Salt

For the pickled pineapple

90ml rice vinegar

25g granulated sugar

¼ pineapple, peeled and diced

For the pickled red onion

1 tbsp granulated sugar

100ml white wine vinegar

2 dried bay leaves

1 garlic clove, halved

1 red onion, cut into slivers

For the rocoto tiger's milk (makes about 220ml)

5mm slice of ginger, bruised

1 garlic clove, halved and bruised

4 coriander sprigs, roughly chopped

Juice of 12 limes, plus extra to taste

½ rocoto pepper or 2 medium-heat red chillies, deseeded and chopped

First, make the pickled pineapple. Put 25ml of water in a small saucepan and add the vinegar and sugar with a pinch of salt. Cook over a low heat for about 2 minutes, stirring, until the sugar has dissolved. Transfer the liquid to a glass container with a lid and allow to cool, then add the pineapple, turning the dice through the syrup mixture to coat. Store in the fridge until you need it.

Next, make the pickled red onion. Put the sugar, vinegar, bay leaves and garlic in a small saucepan with 100ml of water. Bring to the boil over a medium heat, stirring until the sugar has completely dissolved. Add the red onion slivers and allow to cool completely. Transfer to a glass container with a lid and store in the fridge until needed.

To make the rocoto tiger's milk, put the ginger, garlic, coriander and lime juice in a bowl. Allow to infuse for 5 minutes, then strain. Add the rocoto pepper or chilli to the liquid and add ½ teaspoon of salt. Transfer the mixture to a food processor or blender and blitz until smooth. Taste and adjust the salt and lime juice as necessary.

To make the ceviche, put the tuna in a bowl with a pinch of salt. Stir gently, then pour over the rocoto tiger's milk and allow to stand for 2 minutes.

To serve, divide the fish and tiger's milk mixture between 4 plates or dishes and top with equal amounts of the pickled pineapple, pickled red onion, samphire, slices of black radish, black quinoa, and coriander cress or watercress leaves.

Poncho de Palta

SERVES 4

Avocado, Amaranth & Beetroot Poncho. *A poncho is a type of shawl worn by Andina women. As the avocado – known as* palta *in Peru – in this recipe covers many of the ingredients like a blanket, I thought it would be fun to use poncho in the recipe name. It's a dish that surprises – beneath the soft, green avocado lies the bright magenta of the beetroot and amaranth mixture.*

4 asparagus spears

2 ripe avocados

1 quantity of amarillo tiger's milk (see p.74)

A few sweet potato chips (see p.172), to serve

A few amaranth flowers or other edible flowers (optional), to serve

Salt

For the amaranth beetroot

75g amaranth

75g cooked beetroot

1 tbsp amarillo tiger's milk (see p.74)

First, make the amaranth beetroot. Cook the amaranth according to the instructions on page 27, then allow to cool. Purée the beetroot in a food processor or blender, then transfer to a bowl and mix in the amaranth and the 1 tablespoon of tiger's milk. Season with salt.

When you're ready to serve, shave the asparagus very finely with a vegetable peeler. Put the asparagus shavings into iced water and leave for 2–3 minutes – they should curl up a little.

To assemble the dish, halve and peel the avocados, discarding the stones. Put a spoonful of the amaranth and beetroot purée into the well of each avocado half, ensuring that it doesn't go over the edges of the well. Place a plate on top of the cut side of the avocado, then flip it over, so that the avocado is cut-side down with the purée encased within. Pour over some tiger's milk (store any leftover in the fridge – it will keep for up to 2 days, but is best used within 24 hours), season with salt, then top with the asparagus curls. Decorate with sweet potato chips and some edible flowers, if using.

Celador de Camarones

SERVES 4

Prawn Ceviche. *You can make this quick recipe using raw or cooked prawns, but I prefer the traditional Arequipa version, which always uses raw. The freshness of the prawns and the tiger's milk, made using the juice from the discarded prawn shells and lime, make this a memorable dish. This is an ancient recipe that I recently unearthed on a trip to see my favourite* picanteras *in Arequipa.*

4 small sweet potatoes

250g fresh, shell-on prawns

2 red onions, finely sliced

2 large tomatoes, skinned, deseeded and finely sliced

1 rocoto pepper or medium-heat red chillies, deseeded and finely sliced

Juice of 10 limes

1 tbsp red wine vinegar

4 tbsp olive oil

A few coriander or parsley leaves, finely chopped, to serve (optional)

Salt

Preheat the oven to 200°C (gas mark 6). Prick the sweet potatoes all over with a fork, place them on a baking tray, then roast in the oven until tender (about 30–40 minutes).

While the potatoes are roasting, prepare the salad. Peel and devein the prawns and cut out the digestive tract if black. Put the shells and heads (if you have them) into a food processor or blender with a splash of water and blitz until you have a coarse paste. Remove the puréed shells from the processor or blender and push them through a fine sieve to extract as much liquid from them as possible. Set the liquid aside and discard the shells.

Bring a saucepan of water to the boil and blanch the red onion slices for 1 minute only. Drain and cool in iced water, then drain again.

Put the prepared prawns into a large bowl with the red onion, tomato and rocoto pepper or chilli slices. Season well with salt. In a separate bowl, make a dressing by whisking together the lime juice, red wine vinegar, olive oil and reserved prawn liquid until fully combined.

Pour the dressing into the bowl with the prawns and sliced onion and mix thoroughly to combine all the ingredients.

Remove the roasted sweet potatoes from the oven, and, when they are cool enough to handle, peel them and cut them into thick slices. Put equal amounts of the potato on 4 individual serving plates and top each with the prawn mixture, then sprinkle with the chopped herbs, if using. Serve immediately.

Ceviche de Alcachofas

SERVES 4

Artichoke Ceviche. *On a recent trip to the region of Junín, near a town called Concepción, I drove by field after field of beautiful, ripe artichokes. There were women in the fields harvesting and collecting them. This photograph was taken there. Knowing then that the freshest artichokes would be on offer, I stopped by a roadside restaurant and had a perfect artichoke ceviche – the inspiration for this recipe.*

8 artichoke hearts, quartered

2 small parsnips, peeled and cut into thin batons

2 carrots, peeled and cut into thin batons

2 red onions, finely sliced

A small bunch of basil leaves, finely chopped

A few iceberg lettuce leaves, shredded, to serve

For the dressing

2 tbsp olive oil

Juice of 12 limes

2 medium-heat red chillies, deseeded and finely chopped

Salt and freshly ground black pepper

Bring a saucepan of salted water to the boil. Blanch the artichoke hearts and parsnip and carrot batons for 3–4 minutes until just tender, then drain thoroughly and either chill in iced water or cool under running water.

Put the red onion in a large bowl and add the cooled blanched vegetables.

Make the dressing by whisking together the olive oil, lime juice and chilli and season with plenty of salt and pepper. Pour the dressing over the vegetables, sprinkle over the basil leaves and stir very gently to combine.

Serve on a bed of shredded iceberg lettuce.

Tiradito de Conchas y Maracuyá

SERVES 4

Scallop & Passion Fruit Tiradito. *If the US artist Jackson Pollock made ceviches, this would be his masterpiece. Its splashes of colour are dazzling. Unsurprisingly, after its debut, it quickly became one of the most requested dishes on the Andina menu. As well as being gorgeous to look at, the combination of the delicate and sweet scallop, the passion fruit and the squid ink creates a refreshing yet luxurious flavour.*

4 large scallops, trimmed

1 tsp squid ink

A few slices of pickled red onion (see p.82), cut into small pieces, to serve

A few coriander leaves or micro herbs, to serve

Salt

For the passion fruit tiger's milk

5mm slice of ginger, peeled and bruised

1 garlic clove, halved and bruised

4 coriander sprigs, roughly chopped

1 celery stick, roughly chopped

Juice of 10 limes

1 tbsp passion fruit purée

½ tbsp amarillo chilli paste (see p.20)

First, make the passion fruit tiger's milk. Put the ginger, garlic, coriander and celery in a bowl and cover with the lime juice. Allow to infuse for 10 minutes. Strain, then stir in the passion fruit purée and chilli paste. Season with salt.

To assemble the dish, cut the scallops into very thin slices and arrange them over 4 plates. Pour the passion fruit tiger's milk in between the scallops on each plate. Add a few drops of squid ink into the tiger's milk and use a cocktail stick to draw the dots through the liquid to make shapes. Add a few cut slices of pickled red onion and dot over a few coriander leaves. Season only the scallop slices with a little sprinkling of salt, then serve immediately.

Fritos & al Vapor

PAN-FRIED & STEAMED

Puka Picante Vegetariano

SERVES 4

Spicy Olluco, Oca & Beetroot. *On my first trip to the beautiful city of Ayacucho, in the region of the same name, this dish left a big impression on me. Big on colour and flavour, it's popular during Easter in the Andes, as well as for special occasions such as birthdays and weddings. It's also much-loved at Casita Andina, where we think every day is a special occasion.*

200g purple potatoes or regular floury potatoes, skin on and cut into thick slices

200g olluco potatoes or parsnips, unpeeled and cut into thick slices

200g oca potatoes or carrots, unpeeled and cut into thick slices

1 cooked golden baby beetroot, finely sliced, to serve

A few nasturtium, watercress or basil leaves, to decorate

1 tsp beetroot powder or paprika, to decorate (optional)

Salt and freshly ground black pepper

For the puka picante sauce

150g cooked beetroot, diced

1 tbsp olive oil

1 onion, finely chopped

1 garlic clove, finely chopped

1 tsp amarillo chilli paste (see p.20)

2 tsp panca chilli paste (see p.20)

1 tbsp peanut butter

½ tsp ground cumin

50ml single cream or evaporated milk

For the cream cheese sauce

120g smoked cream cheese or goat's milk cream cheese

120ml double cream

Put all the potatoes (or alternatives) into a steamer and cook for about 20 minutes until tender. Drain and set aside to keep warm.

While the potatoes are cooking, make the puka picante sauce. Put the beetroot with 150ml of either beetroot cooking water or fresh water in a food processor or blender and blitz to a purée. Heat the olive oil in a frying pan over a low heat and add the onion. Sauté for about 10 minutes until the onion turns soft and translucent, then add the garlic, chilli pastes and peanut butter. Stir to combine and cook for a further 2–3 minutes until the garlic is soft but hasn't taken on any colour. Add the puréed beetroot to the frying pan, along with the cumin and the single cream or evaporated milk. Season with salt and pepper, then simmer until everything is well combined and heated through. Remove from the heat and set aside.

Make the cream cheese sauce. Put the cream cheese and double cream in a bain marie or a bowl suspended over simmering water. Whisk continuously for about 4–5 minutes until the mixture is silky smooth and thick.

To assemble the dish, divide the puka picante sauce between 4 bowls, then layer on the cream cheese sauce, and then the cooked, drained potatoes (or alternatives). Decorate with the golden beetroot slices and the leaves. Finally, sprinkle over the beetroot powder or paprika, if using.

Lomo de Cordero en Maca

SERVES 4

Maca Lamb Loins. *Peruvians love using maca for desserts and smoothies, but rarely do we use it for a savoury dish – for that reason this recipe is one of my favourites, and much loved by our customers at Casita Andina, too. The combination of maca with olluco tubers, or any nutty potatoes, is just perfect.*

4 lamb chops (about 150g each; use Barnsley or double loin, if you can)

1 quantity of uchucuta sauce (see p.132)

250g potatoes (olluco, anya or new), steamed and sliced, to serve

A generous sprinkling of maca-cancha-panca powder (see below)

Buttermilk, to serve

Amaranth cress or a little chopped parsley, to serve

Salt

For the maca-cancha-panca powder

2 tbsp maca powder

2 tbsp cancha corn or pistachios, lightly crushed

2 tbsp powdered panca chilli or any powdered smoked chilli

For the marinade

1 tbsp achiote oil (see p.146)

3 garlic cloves, crushed

100g panca chilli paste (see p.20)

1 tbsp red wine vinegar

2 tbsp gluten-free soy sauce

First, make the maca-cancha-panca powder by mixing together all the ingredients in a small bowl. Transfer to an airtight jar.

Then, make the marinade. Put all the marinade ingredients in a bowl and mix thoroughly. Add the lamb chops, cover and allow to marinate in the fridge for 3 hours.

When you are ready to cook the lamb, heat a griddle pan until it is too hot to hold your hand over. Brush off any excess marinade from the lamb chops and griddle for a couple of minutes on each side until seared and lightly charred (about 5 minutes). Remove from the heat and leave to rest for 2 minutes. Season with a pinch of salt.

To serve, spread the uchucuta sauce on a serving dish. Place the lamb chops on top of the sauce with the potatoes. Sprinkle a little maca-cancha-panca powder over the chops and potatoes. (Leftover powder will keep in an airtight jar for up to 6 weeks.) Finally, drizzle over a little buttermilk, sprinkle with amaranth cress or chopped parsley and serve immediately.

Tacacho con Setas y Beterraga

SERVES 4

Plantain, Wild Mushrooms & Beetroot. *The region of Huánuco tumbles from the Andes into the Amazon, and tacacho (as here) is a flag bearer for Amazonian cuisine. Wonderful beetroot and wild mushrooms grow in the Andes, too, making this a seamless marriage between the two terrains.*

2 large green plantain, peeled and cut into chunks

Rosemary oil (see below)

Salt and freshly ground black pepper

For the rosemary oil

100ml olive oil

4 garlic cloves, halved

2 rosemary sprigs

For the beetroot purée

150g cooked beetroot

1 tbsp sherry vinegar

1 tbsp rosemary oil

1 tbsp hazelnuts, lightly toasted

For the cheese sauce

100g queso fresco or feta

50ml double cream

For the mushrooms

2 tbsp rosemary oil

2 red onions, cut into wedges

500g seasonal wild mushrooms (ideally, Chanterelle, oyster or wood mushrooms), halved

First, make the rosemary oil. Put the olive oil in a small saucepan and add the garlic and rosemary. Heat over a high heat until bubbles form under the surface, then turn down the heat and leave to simmer very gently for 5 minutes to infuse. Strain the oil and set aside to cool.

Bring a saucepan of salted water to the boil over a high heat. Add the plantain chunks, turn down the heat to low and simmer for about 20 minutes until the plantain is tender. Drain, tip the plantain into a bowl and pour over 50ml of the rosemary oil. Mash to a coarse dough. To make the tacachos, divide the dough into 8 pieces, then roll them into balls and flatten slightly into patties. Season with salt and set aside.

Make the beetroot purée. Put the cooked beetroot in a food processor or blender with the sherry vinegar, rosemary oil and hazelnuts. Season with salt and pepper and blitz to a smooth paste. Season with salt, then set aside and keep warm.

To make the cheese sauce, put the cheese and cream in a small saucepan over a low heat and heat gently until the cheese starts to soften. Transfer to a food processor or blender and blitz until smooth. Set aside and keep warm.

To cook the mushrooms, heat the rosemary oil in a large frying pan over a medium heat. Add the red onion and cook for 5 minutes to give them a head start, then add the mushrooms. Sauté until the mushrooms are glossy and well cooked through (about 6–7 minutes). Season with salt and pepper. Towards the end of the cooking time, briefly add the tacacho patties to the pan, turning to warm through. Remove the pan from the heat.

To assemble the dish, divide the beetroot purée between 4 plates. Top each with 2 tacachos, then pile on the mushrooms and red onions. Drizzle over some of the cheese sauce and serve immediately.

Picante de Mollejas

SERVES 4

Spicy Lamb Sweetbreads. *Panca chilli is native to the Peruvian Andes and provides a mild, aromatic and smoky flavour without any aggressive heat. In this sauce it flavours an exquisite gravy for the creamy, smooth sweetbreads, and blends beautifully with the potatoes.*

600g lamb sweetbreads

150g carapulcra dried potatoes (rinsed, soaked and drained; see p.128); or 300g new potatoes, diced

3 tbsp olive oil

1 small onion, finely chopped

1 garlic clove, finely chopped

65g amarillo chilli paste (see p.20)

1 tbsp peanut butter

15g butter

Salt and freshly ground black pepper

For the marinade

3 tbsp olive oil

3 tbsp panca chilli paste (see p.20)

1 tbsp red wine vinegar

½ tsp dried oregano

½ tsp ground cumin

1 garlic clove, crushed

For the panca glaze

1 tbsp olive oil

2 carrots, finely diced

2 red onions, finely chopped

1 garlic clove, finely chopped

60g panca chilli paste (see p.20)

100ml stout

300ml beef stock

First, soak the sweetbreads in salted water for 5–6 hours, changing the water twice during soaking, to help remove some of the blood.

Bring a saucepan of water to the boil and blanch the soaked sweetbreads for 2 minutes, then remove and plunge into iced water. Trim the sweetbreads, pulling off any fat and membrane.

Make the marinade in a large bowl. Whisk together all the ingredients and season with salt and pepper. Add the sweetbreads to the bowl and stir to coat. Cover and leave to marinate in the fridge for 2 hours.

For the panca glaze, heat the olive oil in a pan over a medium heat and add the carrot and red onion. Sauté for about 10–12 minutes until the onion is golden brown, then add the garlic and chilli paste. Stir to combine, then pour over the stout and the beef stock. Season with salt and pepper and boil until reduced by half and you have a syrupy consistency (about 25 minutes). Purée using a stick blender, then pass the purée through a sieve to give a smooth sauce. Keep warm.

To make the dish, heat 2 tablespoons of the olive oil in a frying pan over a medium heat and add the onion. Sauté for 10 minutes until soft, then add the garlic, chilli paste and peanut butter. Add the potatoes and sauté gently for 10 minutes more. Just cover with water, season and bring to the boil, then reduce the heat to low and simmer for 15–20 minutes until the potatoes are just tender and most of the liquid has evaporated.

Remove the sweetbreads from the marinade and pat dry. Heat the remaining 1 tablespoon of oil in a large frying pan, then add the butter. When it starts to foam, add the sweetbreads and fry for 2–3 minutes on each side until golden brown.

To serve, divide the potato mixture between 4 plates. Top with the sweetbreads and drizzle over the panca glaze.

Shambar con Chicharrón

SERVES 4

La Libertad-style Pork Belly & Pulses. *When I was a child, the journey to visit my grandmother in the Andes was long and tiring. Along the way, though, roadside restaurants served delicious dishes, such as the fortifying soup version of this dish. I love the combination of pulses and crunchy pork belly.*

10ml white wine vinegar

800g pork belly, skin on and scored

1 garlic clove, sliced

1 tsp black peppercorns

A few coriander micro herbs or leaves, to serve

Pork scratching popped corn, to serve

Salt

For the shambar

150g dried chickpeas, soaked overnight and drained

100g split yellow peas, soaked overnight and drained

100g wheatberries, well rinsed

1 tbsp achiote oil (see p.146)

50g smoked gammon knuckle or ham, cubed

1 onion, finely chopped

3 garlic cloves, finely chopped

2 tbsp amarillo chilli paste (see p.20)

1 tsp ground cumin

Preheat the oven to 220°C (gas mark 7). Rub 1 tablespoon of salt and the vinegar over the pork, making sure there is plenty of salt on the skin. Place in a deep roasting tin. Add the garlic slices and peppercorns around the pork, then pour in enough water to cover the meat, but leaving the skin uncovered. Roast in the oven for 30 minutes, then reduce the heat to 180°C (gas mark 4) and cook for a further 2–2½ hours until the skin is crisp. Check the water levels regularly and top up as necessary. Remove from the oven and cut into 4 pieces. Strain the stock, skimming off any fat, and set aside. Keep the pork warm in a low oven.

Meanwhile, start the shambar. Put the drained chickpeas and split peas in a saucepan or casserole with the wheatberries and cover with plenty of water. Bring to the boil over a high heat. Boil fiercely for 10 minutes, then reduce the heat and simmer for 45 minutes to 1 hour, until the chickpeas are cooked, and the split peas are cooked but not mushy. Drain and set aside.

When the pork is cooked you can finish off the shambar. Heat the achiote oil in a large casserole over a medium heat. Turn down the heat and add the smoked gammon or ham and the onion and sauté for about 10 minutes until the onion is soft and translucent. Add the garlic and chilli paste, stir and cook for 2–3 minutes, then add the cooked chickpeas, split peas and wheatberries. Sprinkle over the cumin. Taste the pork stock – if it is very salty, dilute it with water to taste. Add 500ml of the pork stock to the casserole. Bring to the boil, then simmer, uncovered, for 15 minutes until the liquid has reduced to give you a thick sauce.

Using a stick blender, blend the sauce very briefly so that you retain some whole chickpeas. Alternatively, transfer half the mixture to a food processor or blender and pulse a couple of times, then stir the blended sauce back into the unblended half.

Divide the shambar between 4 bowls. Top with the pork, sprinkle with the coriander and popped pork, and serve immediately.

Cuy Frito

SERVES 4

Crackling Guinea Pig or Rabbit. *This ancient Peruvian recipe is cooked in many regions of the Andes. Guinea pig offers a highly sustainable, lean, protein-rich meat packed with healthy fats. The thin skin also makes for a perfect crackling. Guinea pig has been farmed in Peru for thousands of years, since the Inca and pre-Inca civilizations, but you can substitute rabbit (or even chicken), if you prefer.*

1 guinea pig or rabbit, cleaned

Vegetable oil, for frying

50ml rocoto llactan sauce (see p.47)

A green salad, to serve

4 large potatoes, boiled and sliced, to serve

Salt

Cut the guinea pig or rabbit in half widthways. Take each piece and press down on the backbone to flatten it out a little. Sprinkle generously with salt.

Take a deep frying pan that is large enough to hold the splayed guinea pig or rabbit and fill it with oil to about 2cm deep. Heat the oil to about 120°C over a low–medium heat. Add the meat, place a plate on top and weigh it down with some tins. Cook the meat gently for about 15–20 minutes, turning once during the cooking, until the guinea pig or rabbit is cooked through without having taken on much colour.

Remove the meat from the pan and set aside to drain thoroughly on kitchen paper. You can cook it again immediately, or allow it to cool and store until you are ready to cook and eat it. (Keep the oil to use again in the next step.)

Reheat the oil over a medium–high heat to about 180°C. Season the guinea pig or rabbit with salt again and fry, weighted, for about 5 minutes on each side until the skin is crisp and brown – and very crunchy. Remove from the oil and drain again on kitchen paper, then serve hot, with the rocoto llactan sauce, green salad and potatoes on the side.

Tacu Tacu Quechua

SERVES 4

Aubergine Quechua Tacu Tacu. *Flavouring an aubergine to provide an exciting dish is not just the preserve of Italian, Lebanese, Greek or Turkish cooking. Proof of that is right here. Bringing in influences from all corners of Peru, but using many Andina ingredients, this dish has tons of character and personality with its variety of textures and spices.*

Olive oil, for frying

2 aubergines, sliced into 2cm-thick chunks or rounds

50g queso fresco or feta, crumbled, to serve

A few coriander leaves, to serve

Salt

For the sauce

60ml olive oil

4 garlic cloves, crushed

60ml white wine vinegar

175g panca chilli paste (see p.20)

60g rocoto pepper paste (see p.62)

A few coriander sprigs, finely chopped

A few mint sprigs, finely chopped

For the quinoa tacu tacu

1 tbsp olive oil

1 small red onion, finely chopped

1 tomato, finely chopped

100g cooked butter beans

1 tbsp amarillo chilli paste (see p.20)

1 tsp ground cumin

65g black quinoa, cooked (see p.64)

First, make the sauce. Heat the olive oil in a large frying pan over a medium heat and add the garlic. Sauté for 2 minutes until the garlic is very lightly cooked. Add the vinegar, chilli and pepper pastes and herbs, then season with salt. Simmer over a very low heat for 10 minutes, stirring, until everything is well combined. If it starts to look dry at any point, add a splash of water. Remove from the heat and set aside.

Next, make the quinoa tacu tacu. Heat the olive oil in a frying pan over a low heat. Add the onion and sauté for about 5 minutes until softened, then add the tomato, butter beans, chilli paste and cumin. Continue to cook for a further 5 minutes until everything is well combined and any liquid from the tomatoes has evaporated. Remove from the heat.

Mash the butter bean mixture roughly with a fork – you need to keep some texture – then mix in the quinoa. Allow to cool, then divide the mixture into 4 equal portions and shape into long (aubergine-shaped) patties.

To make the dish, coat the base of a large frying pan with olive oil. Fry the aubergine pieces over a medium heat for 6–8 minutes, turning until golden on all sides. Remove from the pan and set aside to drain on kitchen paper. Keep warm. You may have to do this in several batches. When you've fried all the aubergine slices, add them to the sauce and reheat until piping hot.

To fry the quinoa tacu tacu patties, heat a little olive oil in a large frying pan over a medium heat. Add the patties and fry for 3–4 minutes on each side until lightly browned all over.

To assemble the dish, place each patty on a plate and top with the aubergine and sauce. Sprinkle over some crumbled queso fresco or feta and a few coriander leaves and serve immediately.

Olluquito con Charqui

SERVES 4

Jerky with Olluco. *The origins of this recipe date back 4,000 years, making this one of the most ancient dishes in the Andes. A favourite of the Incas, it uses two of the Andes region's most beloved ingredients – alpaca charqui and olluco potatoes. Beef or lamb jerky make easy substitutions for the charqui that don't compromise the traditional flavour.*

200g alpaca charqui or beef or lamb jerky, or 300g roast meat (beef, lamb or pork)

4 tbsp olive oil, plus extra for frying the roast meat (if using)

1 large red onion, finely chopped

6 garlic cloves, crushed

2½ tbsp panca chilli paste (see p.20)

1 tbsp amarillo chilli paste (see p.20)

1 tsp ground white pepper

1 tsp ground cumin

750g olluco or small new potatoes, thinly sliced

A small bunch of parsley, finely chopped, to serve

Salt and freshly ground black pepper

If using the alpaca charqui or beef or lamb jerky, cover with warm water and leave to soak for 1 hour, changing the water every 15–20 minutes. Drain and set aside. If using the roast meat, heat a little oil in a frying pan and fry until very crisp and well browned. Set aside.

Heat the 4 tablespoons of olive oil in a large, lidded frying pan or casserole over a medium heat and add the onion. Sauté for 8–10 minutes until very soft, then add the garlic, chilli pastes, white pepper and cumin. Cook for a further 2–3 minutes until everything is well combined. Add the olluco or new potato slices and charqui or roast meat, along with about 150ml of water. Cover and cook gently over a low heat for about 35–40 minutes until the olluco or new potato slices are tender. Season with salt and pepper to taste. Serve immediately, sprinkled with the chopped parsley.

Hamburguesa de Quinua

MAKES 6 BURGERS

Quinoa Burgers. *Tired of tasteless veggie burgers, I set about making the best meat-free burger I could. My aim was to beat the taste and texture of a straightforward gourmet beef burger – whether or not I've achieved that is something only you can decide, but this dish is now one of the most frequently requested at Andina.*

1 tbsp vegetable oil, plus extra for shallow frying

1 small red onion, finely chopped

1 garlic clove, crushed

80g amarillo chilli paste (see p.20)

120g mixed quinoa (red, black and white), cooked (see p.64)

20g maca powder or plain flour, plus extra flour for dusting

60g queso fresco or feta

30g vegetarian Parmesan-like hard cheese, grated

½ tsp ground cumin

2 eggs, beaten

80g panko breadcrumbs

1 quantity of amarillo chilli mayonnaise (see p.30)

6 large poppy seed buns, to serve

2 little gem lettuces, to serve

1 quantity of salsa criolla (see p.120), to serve

Salt and freshly ground black pepper

For the yogurt dressing

1 green papaya or cucumber

125ml Greek yogurt

1 kiwi, peeled and chopped

1 tbsp finely chopped mint leaves

Heat the vegetable oil in a frying pan over a medium heat and add the onion. Sauté for about 7–8 minutes until soft, then add the garlic and chilli paste. Cook for a further 2–3 minutes until the paste starts to separate, then remove from the heat and allow to cool completely.

Combine the quinoa and the cooled onion and chilli paste in a bowl with the maca powder or flour and cheeses. Add the cumin, season well with salt and pepper and combine. Divide into 6 patties and chill in the fridge for at least 1 hour to firm up.

Meanwhile, make the yogurt dressing. Peel, deseed and grate the papaya or cucumber, then drain the grated flesh to get rid of any excess water. Mix the flesh with the remaining ingredients and season with salt and pepper. Set aside.

Cook the quinoa burgers. Dust each burger generously with flour and pat off any excess. Dip in the beaten egg and coat in the breadcrumbs. To cook, heat some vegetable oil in a large frying pan and shallow fry each burger for 5–6 minutes on each side until golden brown and heated through.

To assemble, halve each bun and spread some amarillo chilli mayonnaise on the cut sides, then toast in a large frying pan, spread-side down for a few moments, just to soften the bread a little. Remove from the pan. Spoon a little yogurt dressing on the bottom half of each burger bun, top with 1 or 2 little gem leaves and then the burger, and finish off with a spoonful of the salsa criolla and the burger bun on top. Serve immediately.

Rocoto Relleno Vegetariano

SERVES 4

Stuffed Rocoto Peppers. *Don't be fooled by the humble appearance: rocoto peppers are full of fiery Andina spirit. This traditional dish comes from the region of Arequipa where the method of triple-boiling the rocotos before stuffing, and then topping them with smooth, creamy cheese, leaves you with a far more easy-going heat. Always use fresh, rather than frozen rocoto, as frozen will collapse as they cook.*

4 rocoto peppers or large
red peppers

90ml white wine vinegar

90g granulated sugar

For the filling

1 tbsp olive oil

40g butter

500g wild mushrooms, sliced

Leaves from 4 thyme sprigs,
finely chopped

2 garlic cloves, finely chopped

2 tsp red chilli flakes, if using red
peppers rather than rocoto

250ml double cream

120g queso fresco or feta, crumbled

Salt and freshly ground
black pepper

Preheat the oven to 180°C (gas mark 4).

Carefully cut out a cap from the top of each of the rocoto or red peppers and pull out the core and seeds. Reserve the caps if you wish. Put the peppers in a large saucepan and cover with water. Add one-third of the vinegar and sugar, then bring to the boil and simmer for 3 minutes. Drain, replace the peppers in the pan and repeat the process twice until you have used up all the sugar and vinegar. Set aside the peppers.

To make the filling, heat the olive oil and butter in a large frying pan over a medium heat. Add the mushrooms, thyme, garlic and chilli flakes (if using), and season with salt and pepper. Sauté for 10 minutes until the mushrooms are cooked through. Pour in the double cream and allow to simmer for a couple of minutes, then remove from the heat and allow to cool.

When the mushroom mixture has cooled down, spoon it into the peppers, then top with equal amounts of the cheese. Put the stuffed peppers into a small baking dish or tin – you want a fairly snug fit to help the peppers stay upright. Replace the reserved caps on the peppers, if you wish. Bake in the oven for about 25 minutes until the filling is piping hot and the cheese is melted and lightly browned. Serve immediately.

Chaufa Huánuco

SERVES 4

Chifa-style Tempeh & Quinoa. *Chinese migrants arrived in Peru in the 19th century and, among other businesses, they established restaurants called Chifas that used Chinese cooking techniques with native Peruvian ingredients. Huánuco has its fair share of Chifas and this dish is my way to honour that fusion and Chinese–Peruvian tradition.*

500g tempeh, cut into 2cm cubes

2 tbsp vegetable oil, plus extra for deep frying

30g cornflour

1 large onion, finely chopped

½ red pepper, finely chopped

100g sweetcorn kernels, blanched

2 tbsp dry sherry or pisco

2 medium-heat red chillies, finely chopped

100g peas, blanched

90g black quinoa, cooked (see p.64)

1 tbsp light gluten-free soy sauce

2 tsp sesame oil

2 beaten eggs

4 spring onions, finely chopped

A small bunch of coriander, leaves and stalks finely chopped

A few tarragon sprigs, leaves and stalks finely chopped

1 tbsp yacon or maple syrup

For the marinade

2 tbsp panca chilli paste (see p.20)

3 tbsp light gluten-free soy sauce

3 garlic cloves, crushed

2cm piece of ginger, peeled and finely chopped

First, make the marinade. In a large bowl, whisk together the chilli paste and soy sauce, then stir in the garlic and ginger.

Add the tempeh to the bowl with the marinade and stir to coat. Cover and marinate in the fridge for at least 5 hours, or overnight if possible.

When you're ready to cook, drain the tempeh, reserving the marinade. To deep fry the tempeh, pour vegetable oil into a deep saucepan, or deep-fat fryer, so that it comes about halfway up the sides and heat to about 180°C. Pat the tempeh dry with kitchen paper, then dust with the cornflour. Fry, in batches if necessary, for about 2–3 minutes until crisp and golden brown. Remove from the oil with a slotted spoon and set aside to drain on kitchen paper.

Heat the vegetable oil in a large frying pan or wok over a high heat. Add the onion, red pepper and sweetcorn. Add the sherry or pisco and set alight quickly to flambée the ingredients. When the flames have subsided, add the red chilli, peas and quinoa to the pan and sauté for 2–3 minutes, stirring continuously, until everything is well combined. Add the soy sauce and sesame oil, along with a dash of the reserved marinade, and stir through to combine. Tip the contents of the pan into a bowl. Heat a touch of oil in the pan and add the beaten eggs, spring onion and all the herbs. Stir until the eggs have cooked and everything is fully combined. Roughly chop them up with a wooden spoon, then reintroduce the stir-fried ingredients and mix everything together. Take the pan off the heat.

Heat the remaining marinade in a small saucepan over a low heat with the yacon or maple syrup. To serve, divide the quinoa mixture between 4 shallow bowls and arrange the deep-fried tempeh on top. Drizzle over the warm marinade and serve immediately.

Pachamanca

SERVES 8

Fire, Stone & Earth Ancient Cooking. *This dish and its cooking technique are among the oldest in the Andes and some of the best examples are found in the region of Pasco. Traditionally made to celebrate special occasions, pachamanca will feed a small gathering. You'll need about ten large banana leaves, a pile of large stones and about five hessian sacks.*

1kg pork belly, on the bone, cut into thick slices

8 chicken thighs, on the bone, skin on

8 large potatoes

4 sweet potatoes

1 large cassava, peeled and cut into large chunks

400g choclo corn

400g broad beans

400ml rocoto llactan sauce (see p.47), to serve

For the marinade

300ml olive oil

100ml red wine vinegar

100ml chicha (see p.199) or dry cider

200g huacatay herb paste (see p.132)

3 garlic cloves, crushed

½ tsp dried oregano

½ tsp ground cumin

Salt and freshly ground black pepper

First, make the marinade. Whisk together all the ingredients in a small jug and season with salt and pepper.

Put the pork belly and chicken thighs in a large bowl and pour over the marinade. Rub the marinade into the meat. Cover and leave to marinate in the fridge overnight. Remove the meat from the fridge at least 1 hour before you start cooking.

Prepare the pit. Dig a 60cm-square and 50cm-deep hole, reserving the removed earth. Moisten the sides of the hole, patting to make them firm. When the sides are dry, use kindling and a few logs to make a fire in the bottom. Put a metal grate or rack over the top of the hole and cover with 15–20 large, clean stones or pebbles (each needs to be about the size of a large fist). You will need enough stones to (eventually) almost fill the hole. Allow the stones to heat up for about 30 minutes until very hot.

Wearing fire-proof gloves, pile the hot stones onto a metal tray. Remove the grate or rack and put a single layer of stones at the bottom of the hole on top of what remains of your fire. Cover with a layer of banana leaves. Brush the marinade from the meat and place it on top of the banana leaves. Cover the meat with more banana leaves and add another layer of hot stones. Put the potatoes, sweet potatoes and cassava on top, then more banana leaves. Pile in the corn and broad beans and cover with a final layer of banana leaves and a few hessian sacks so that everything is completely covered. Cover over with the reserved earth to fill the hole and leave for 2 hours until everything is cooked.

To serve, remove the earth carefully, then the sacks. Remove the cooked food layer by layer to warm serving platters and serve immediately with the rocoto llactan sauce.

Pato Sampa

SERVES 4

Humble Duck. *Duck appears in hundreds of great recipes across the various regions of the Peruvian Andes. In this recipe there are elements and ingredients of traditional northern Andina cuisine, creatively combined with seasonal ingredients. For me, the flavours of the marinated duck together with the sweet potato are simply exquisite.*

4 duck breasts, skin on

2 small sweet potatoes

50ml chicken stock

40g black quinoa, cooked
(see p.64)

1 tbsp olive oil

2 handfuls of baby salad leaves,
to serve

Salt and freshly ground black
pepper

For the marinade

50g garlic purée

40ml red wine vinegar

150ml freshly squeezed orange juice

120g panca chilli paste (see p.20)

2 tbsp huacatay herb paste
(see p.132)

½ tsp ground cumin

½ tsp salt

First, make the marinade by mixing all the marinade ingredients in a large bowl.

Slash the skin on the duck breasts lightly and place the breasts in the bowl with the marinade. Rub the marinade into the meat, then cover and marinate in the fridge for at least 3 hours.

Preheat the oven to 200°C (gas mark 6). Prick the sweet potatoes all over with a fork, then place them on a baking tray and put them in the oven to roast for about 30–40 minutes until soft. When the potatoes are cool enough to handle, halve each potato, scoop the flesh from the skin, place it in a bowl, season well with salt and pepper and mash until smooth. Set aside and keep warm.

When you are ready to cook the duck, remove it from the marinade and pat dry, then set aside. Put the marinade in a small saucepan with the chicken stock, over a medium heat. Bring to the boil, then turn down the heat to low and simmer for about 20 minutes until the liquid has reduced by half. Remove from the heat and stir in the quinoa.

Meanwhile, heat the olive oil in a large frying pan until hot. Sear the duck breasts, skin-side down, for about 6 minutes, then turn over and cook for another 2 minutes until the underside is seared. Remove the duck from the pan and set aside on a warm plate to rest.

Divide the sweet potato mash between 4 plates, spreading it across each plate. Cut each duck breast into 2.5cm-thick slices and arrange the slices equally over the mash, then pour over the quinoa sauce. Serve immediately with the baby salad leaves.

A la Parrilla, al Horno & Asados

GRILLED, BAKED & ROASTED

Trucha a la Parrilla de La Oroya

SERVES 4

La Oroya Fish & Chips. *La Oroya, a city deep in the heart of the Andes, was the first place in Peru to farm trout. When I was a child, my father would visit La Oroya for work, and he also loved a good British fish and chips! If he were alive today, I'm sure he would appreciate my Andina alternative.*

4 small or 2 large trout, cleaned

30g butter, melted

Salt and freshly ground black pepper

For the marinade

4 tbsp olive oil

1 red onion, finely chopped

6 garlic cloves, crushed

2 tbsp panca chilli paste (see p.20)

½ tsp ground cumin

A few coriander leaves, chopped

For the cassava chips

1 cassava, peeled

Vegetable oil, for deep frying

For the broad bean mash

400g broad beans

50ml double cream

15g butter

A few mint sprigs, finely chopped

First, make the marinade. Heat the olive oil in a frying pan over a medium heat. Add the red onion and sauté for 10 minutes until the onion has softened, then add the garlic and cook for a further 2 minutes until the garlic has softened slightly. Remove from the heat, allow to cool, then transfer to a food processor. Add the chilli paste, cumin and coriander. Season, then blitz until smooth.

Cut slashes in the trout skin and place the fish on a baking tray. Rub the marinade over the trout, cover and marinate for 1 hour. Preheat the oven to 200°C (gas mark 6) or prepare a barbecue.

Make the cassava chips. Put the cassava in a saucepan and cover with water, then bring to the boil over a high heat. Add 1 teaspoon of salt to the water, then simmer for 20–30 minutes until the cassava is tender – it will also look translucent. Drain thoroughly. As soon as it is cool enough to handle, break it up into large pieces, remove the stringy bits and cut into rough chips. Half-fill a large saucepan with vegetable oil, or use a deep-fat fryer, and heat the oil to about 180°C. Fry the cassava in batches until piping hot and golden, then remove and set aside to drain on kitchen paper. Keep warm.

To make the broad bean mash, bring a small saucepan of salted water to the boil. Add the beans and simmer for 5 minutes until softened. Drain, then pop half the beans out of their skins and put them with the unpopped beans in a food processor or blender. Warm the cream slightly in a small saucepan, then add to the processor or blender with the butter. Pulse the mixture to a coarse purée, then stir through the chopped mint and season well with salt. Heat through gently if necessary before serving.

Brush the trout with the melted butter and bake in the oven for 20 minutes until the skin is light brown and crisp and the fish is cooked. Alternatively, grill on a hot barbecue for about 6 minutes on each side. Serve with the cassava chips and broad bean mash.

Pastel de Alcachofas

SERVES 6–8

Artichoke Pie. *People in the Andes love a good pie as anything wrapped in pastry is portable and can be eaten cold or hot. You can find artichoke or chard pies in bakeries and cafés throughout the Andes. A good slice of this artichoke pie makes great food-on-the-go, but it's also perfect eaten at home with an Ensalada Sierra (see p.64) or Solterito (p.66).*

3 tbsp olive oil

½ red onion, finely chopped

2 garlic cloves, finely chopped

2 tbsp plain flour

200ml full-fat milk

12 artichoke hearts, roughly chopped

2½ tbsp breadcrumbs

50g vegetarian Parmesan-like hard cheese, grated

2 eggs, beaten

3 handfuls of spinach leaves

1 egg, beaten, for egg wash

Salad leaves, to serve

Salt and freshly ground black pepper

For the pastry

200g plain flour, plus extra for rolling

90g butter, cubed and chilled

1 egg yolk

75ml iced water

First, make the pastry. Rub together the flour and butter with a pinch of salt until the mixture resembles breadcrumbs, then work in the egg yolk and water. When you have a smooth dough, wrap it up in clingfilm and put it in the fridge to chill for 30 minutes.

Meanwhile, make the pie filling. Heat the olive oil in a large, deep-sided frying pan over a low heat. Add the onion and sauté for about 10 minutes until soft and translucent, then add the garlic and cook for a further 2–3 minutes to soften. Add the flour and stir until it has combined with the olive oil, then gradually incorporate the milk in the same way as you would when making a béchamel. When all the milk is incorporated, allow the liquid to simmer for 10 minutes, stirring often, until thickened.

Remove the pan from the heat and stir in the artichoke, breadcrumbs, cheese and eggs. Season well with salt and pepper and allow to cool. When the filling has cooled down, transfer to a food processor or blender, add the spinach and blitz until the texture is a little smoother.

Preheat the oven to 180°C (gas mark 4). Remove the pastry from the fridge and divide it into 2 pieces, one slightly larger than the other. Dust your work surface with flour and roll out the larger piece of pastry to a circle of about 25cm in diameter. Use this to line a 22–23cm diameter ceramic flan dish. Add the filling, then trim the pastry and brush the exposed rim with some egg wash. Roll out the remaining piece of pastry and use a sharp knife to cut out leaf shapes, arranging them in 2 concentric circles around the top of the filling, as shown, leaving a central hole to allow steam to escape. You'll need about 35 leaf shapes altogether. Brush the leaves well with the remaining egg wash.

Bake the pie in the oven for about 40–45 minutes until the crust is a deep golden brown and the filling is piping hot. Serve hot or cold with a salad on the side.

Loche con Chancaca

SERVES 4

Squash with Chancaca Syrup. *This is a simple side dish that features sweet, savoury, bitter and sour flavours all marrying beautifully into one. The creaminess of the queso fresco balances the sweet syrup and the grilled edges of the squash. If you are short on time, you can use yacon or maple syrup rather than making the chancaca syrup.*

2 tbsp olive oil

1 butternut squash, upper part only (about 600g), peeled and cut lengthways into 4 wedges

50g queso fresco or feta, crumbled

Salt and freshly ground black pepper

For the chancaca syrup (makes about 50ml)

15g panela, palm sugar, jaggery or light soft brown sugar

¼ limo chilli or 1 medium-heat red chilli, deseeded and chopped

¼ tsp ground ginger

1 tbsp freshly squeezed orange juice

3 black peppercorns

For the salsa criolla

1 red onion, halved and thinly sliced

1 small tomato, halved and thinly sliced

1 tbsp lime juice

1 tbsp olive oil

A few coriander leaves, finely chopped

Preheat the oven to 180°C (gas mark 4).

Heat the olive oil in a large frying pan or an ovenproof skillet over a medium heat. Add the squash and sear for about 2 minutes on each side until well charred all over. If you are not using an ovenproof skillet, transfer the squash to a roasting tin. Put the seared squash in the oven to roast for about 20 minutes until tender.

Meanwhile, make the chancaca syrup. Put all the ingredients into a small saucepan with 10ml of water over a medium heat. Bring to the boil, then reduce the heat to low and simmer very gently until the sugar has dissolved and the liquid has reduced to a syrupy consistency (about 10 minutes). Remove from the heat and strain the liquid into a bowl.

To make the salsa criolla, combine all the ingredients in a bowl and season well with salt and pepper.

When the squash is ready, put 1 wedge on each plate and pour over equal amounts of the chancaca syrup. Top with some salsa criolla and finish with a sprinkling of crumbled cheese. Serve immediately.

Alcachofa a la Parrilla

SERVES 4

Grilled Artichoke with Huacatay Hollandaise. *I love the flavour in the charred edges of an artichoke – and the creamy herb dip in this dish is its match made in heaven. Globe artichokes grow in the regions of Cusco and Huancayo and locals use them in a variety of speciality dishes. They taste delicious, of course, but they are also full of antioxidants, fibre and vitamins, making them healthy, too.*

4 large globe artichokes

Juice of ½ lemon

About 500ml olive oil, for confiting, plus extra to griddle

2 star anise

A small bunch of thyme

3 garlic cloves, halved

Pared zest of ½ lemon

Pared zest of ½ orange

2 tbsp cancha corn or cashew nuts, lightly crushed, to serve

½ quantity of huacatay hollandaise (see p.25), warmed, to serve

Prepare the artichokes by removing the tough, spiky outer leaves – keep going until you get to more tender, lighter-coloured leaves. Trim off the leaves around the stem and heart. Cut the artichokes in half and remove each 'choke' – this is the fibrous bit that sits on top of the heart. Then, dip the artichokes in the lemon juice to stop them turning black.

Put the artichokes in a saucepan so that they fit snugly, then pour over the 500ml of olive oil. Add the star anise, thyme, garlic and citrus zests. Put the pan over a medium heat and slowly heat the oil until it is bubbling – about 5 minutes. Cook the artichokes for about 15–20 minutes until the stems are tender – check by piercing them with the tip of a sharp knife. When they are ready, remove the pan from the heat and set the artichokes aside to cool in the pan.

When you are ready to eat, heat a griddle until it is too hot to hold your hand over. Drain the artichokes and blot them with kitchen paper. Brush them with olive oil, then place them cut-side down on the griddle and cook for about 2–3 minutes until they develop char lines. Serve sprinkled with the crushed cancha or cashews and drizzled with the huacatay hollandaise.

Bistec Escabechado

SERVES 4

Escabeche Steak. *The marinade in this recipe takes the steak to the next level. A post-workout favourite for our customers at Andina, this dish is lean and rich in protein, and with the creamy corn giving it a final, indulgent twist, it's unforgettable.*

4 fillet steaks (about 150g each)

A few micro herbs, to decorate

Salt and ground black pepper

For the marinade

150ml gluten-free soy sauce

2 tsp garlic paste

20ml red wine vinegar

½ tsp dried oregano

¼ tsp ground cumin

For the choclo corn cream

1 tbsp olive oil

½ onion, finely chopped

½ tbsp amarillo chilli paste (see p.20)

200g sweetcorn kernels

50g choclo corn or sweetcorn

¼ tsp ground cumin

120ml full-fat milk

½ tsp white wine vinegar

For the escabeche

1 tbsp olive oil

1 small red onion, chopped

½ red pepper, chopped

1 garlic clove, finely chopped

1 amarillo chilli, finely chopped, or 2 tbsp amarillo chilli paste (p.20)

2 tbsp pisco or vodka

2 tsp red wine vinegar

1 tsp yacon syrup or caster sugar

First, make the marinade by mixing all the ingredients together in a large bowl. Add the steaks to the bowl, coat, cover and marinate in the fridge for at least 5 hours.

Remove the steaks from the fridge and take them out of the marinade 30 minutes before you intend to start cooking. When you are ready, first make the choclo corn cream. Heat the olive oil in a saucepan over a medium heat. Add the onion and sauté for about 10 minutes until softened, then add the chilli paste. Cook, stirring, for 2–3 minutes more, then add the sweetcorn, choclo (or additional sweetcorn) and cumin. Sauté for 1 minute, stirring, then add the milk and bring almost to the boil. Reduce the heat to low and simmer for 5 minutes until the liquid has reduced by a third. Add the white wine vinegar, then use a stick blender to blitz to a rough purée. Set aside and keep warm.

Next, make the escabeche. Heat the olive oil in a saucepan over a medium heat. Add the red onion and red pepper and sauté for 5–6 minutes until they have started to take on a little colour and are beginning to soften. Add the garlic and chilli or chilli paste and sauté for 2–3 minutes until the garlic has started to soften but not taken on any colour. Add the pisco or vodka, red wine vinegar and syrup or sugar and season. Bring to the boil, then reduce the heat to low and simmer for about 5 minutes until the liquid has reduced by at least half and is syrupy.

Blot the steaks with kitchen paper and sprinkle each one with salt on both sides. Heat a griddle until it is too hot to hold your hand over, then sear for 1 minute on each side, then cook for a further 2–3 minutes for rare, 5 minutes for medium–rare and 6–7 minutes for medium, turning every 30 seconds or so. Remove from the heat and leave to rest for 5 minutes. Slice the steak and serve on individual serving plates on a bed of the choclo corn cream, with the escabeche on the side or over the top of the steak, and decorate with a few micro herbs.

El Lechoncito de Mamita Naty

SERVES 10–12

Mamita Naty's Roast Suckling Pig. *If you love pork, this simple suckling pig recipe, which is inspired by my granny's version, will make your wildest dreams come true. It's a sharing dish that can go very far, but do measure your oven before you buy the meat and ask your butcher to cut the pig in half if necessary. It's delicious with roast potatoes and veg, or simply shredded and served in a toasted bun.*

1 whole suckling pig (about 5–7kg)

16 medium-heat red chillies

1 tbsp plain flour

Salt and freshly ground black pepper

For the marinade

300ml orange juice

30 physalis, puréed

125ml pisco or vodka

8 garlic cloves, crushed

5 tbsp ground cumin

Zest of 2 oranges

For the apple sauce

1kg cooking apples, peeled, cored and roughly sliced

2 star anise

2 cinnamon sticks

4 medium-heat red chillies, deseeded and finely chopped

3 tbsp yacon syrup or light soft brown sugar

Combine all the marinade ingredients and season with salt and pepper. Then, cut deep slits all over the pig, about 3–4cm apart. Put the marinade and the pig into a large bag, then double bag for good measure and leave it in the fridge for 24 hours, turning the pig within the bag at least once during this time.

Remove the pig from the fridge for 2–3 hours before you want to cook, to return it to room temperature. Just before you are ready to roast, preheat the oven to 220°C (gas mark 7).

Put the suckling pig on a very large roasting tray and season heavily with salt. Wrap the head, trotters and tail in foil, then place in the oven for 15–20 minutes until the skin turns golden.

Lower the oven temperature to 150°C (gas mark 2) and roast the pig for a further 3–4 hours depending on the weight (3 hours for a 5kg pig; 3½ hours for a 6kg pig; 4 hours for a 7kg pig). After the first 2 hours, check the pig every 30 minutes to make sure it isn't browning too quickly – if it looks in danger of burning, reduce the oven temperature slightly. Baste regularly throughout roasting. Then, 30 minutes before the end of the cooking time, unwrap the head, trotters and tail and add the whole chillies to the tray. The pig is cooked when the juices run clear. Then, remove the tray from the oven, transfer the pig to a warmed serving platter, loosely cover with foil and leave it to rest. Spoon off any fat from the roasting tin and strain off the pan juices. Sprinkle the flour into the tin, scrape up any brown bits, then gradually add back the juices to make a gravy over a medium heat. Check the seasoning and adjust if necessary.

To make the apple sauce, put the apple in a saucepan with the spices, chillies and syrup or sugar over a low heat, then add 150ml of water. Simmer for 5–6 minutes until the sugar (if using) has dissolved and the apples have collapsed into a sauce. Remove the spices just before serving alongside the whole pig.

Pulpo Chancón

SERVES 4

The Studious Octopus. *This dramatic and fun recipe cooks up a Saturday-night delight at Andina – it's also a stunner for a dinner party. In Peru,* chancón *is a slang word meaning 'studious', but it also sounds like chancaca, the luscious syrup that you pour over the octopus in this dish – hence, we have the name 'the studious octopus'.*

1 tbsp lime juice

3 garlic cloves, crushed

½ red onion, finely chopped

1 small octopus (preferably frozen and defrosted)

120ml chancaca syrup (see p.120) or yacon syrup, to serve

1 quantity of salsa criolla (see p.120), to serve

Salt and freshly ground black pepper

For the butter bean purée

1 tbsp olive oil

½ red onion, finely chopped

1 tomato, finely chopped

2 tbsp amarillo chilli paste (see p.20)

1 tin of butter beans (about 235g drained weight)

70g lucuma purée, or 1 heaped tbsp lucuma powder mixed with 50ml water

Put the lime juice, garlic and red onion in a large saucepan and add 3 litres of water. Bring to the boil over a high heat and add 1 teaspoon of salt. Use kitchen tongs to dip the octopus 3 times in the liquid, then submerge and release them into the water – the dipping will help the tentacles to curl up in a pleasing way.

Reduce the heat to low, cover the pan and simmer the octopus for about 1 hour, or until tender, then remove, rinse and allow to cool.

Meanwhile, make the butter bean purée. Heat the olive oil in a large frying pan over a medium heat. Add the red onion and sauté for about 10 minutes until soft and translucent. Add the tomato and chilli paste and cook for 2–3 minutes until the tomato has softened and collapsed into the sauce. Add the butter beans and lucuma and heat through. Season with salt and pepper, then transfer to a food processor or blender and blitz to a coarse purée.

Heat a griddle pan until it is too hot to hold your hand over. Cut up the octopus, leaving the tentacles whole and the body cut to a similar thickness as the base of each tentacle. Griddle the octopus pieces for about 8 minutes, turning until crisp and richly brown all over. Divide the butter bean purée between 4 individual serving plates, then arrange equal portions of the octopus on top. Drizzle over the chancaca syrup and serve with the salsa criolla alongside.

Corderito Tierno

SERVES 4

Tender Lamb. *Marinating lamb cutlets tenderizes them, which prepares them well for cooking on a griddle pan or a barbecue. Remember to prepare everything else before you start to cook the lamb, so that you're ready to serve as soon as the meat is ready.*

8 lamb chops or cutlets
(about 100g each)

160g carapulcra dried potatoes;
or 320g new potatoes, peeled
and quartered

2 tbsp olive oil

½ small onion, finely chopped

2 garlic cloves, finely chopped

65g amarillo chilli paste (see p.20)

1 tbsp peanut butter

Salt and ground black pepper

For the marinade

50ml olive oil

3 tbsp panca chilli paste (see p.20)

20ml white wine vinegar

2 garlic cloves, crushed

½ tsp dried oregano

¼ tsp ground cumin

½ tsp salt

For the Túpac Amaru salsa

2 tbsp olive oil

2 tsp red wine vinegar

1 tsp gluten-free soy sauce

½ tsp finely chopped limo chilli
or 1 medium-heat red chilli, finely
chopped

100–120g huacatay herb paste
(see p.132)

The day before you intend to cook, whisk together all the marinade ingredients in a large bowl. Add the lamb, turning the chops or cutlets over in the marinade until well covered, then massage the marinade into the meat with your hands. Cover and marinate in the fridge for 24 hours.

On the day of cooking, first prepare the dried potatoes, if using. Wash them several times until the water runs clear, indicating that most of the starch has been removed. Put the potatoes in a bowl, cover with cold water and leave to soak for 2–3 hours. Remove the lamb from the fridge 1 hour before you intend to start cooking, to bring it up to room temperature.

Meanwhile, make the salsa. Put all the ingredients in a bowl and season with salt, then mix thoroughly and set aside.

To cook the potatoes, heat the olive oil in a large saucepan over a low–medium heat. Add the onion and sauté for 10 minutes until the onion is very soft and translucent. Add the garlic and chilli paste and cook for a further 2–3 minutes until the garlic has softened. Drain the carapulcra potatoes, if using. Add these or the quartered, raw new potatoes to the pan. Sauté for 2–3 minutes until the potatoes have taken on the flavour and colour of the chilli paste, then add the peanut butter and mix well. Add just enough water to cover the potatoes. Bring to the boil, then reduce the heat to low and simmer for 10–15 minutes until tender.

While the potatoes are cooking, heat a griddle pan or frying pan until too hot to hold your hand over (or heat a barbecue). Griddle the lamb pieces for 2 minutes on each side, then remove them from the pan and leave to rest on a board for at least 5 minutes.

To serve, divide the potatoes between 4 plates. Top each with 2 lamb chops or cutlets per person, then drizzle over the salsa.

Empanada Shoreditch

MAKES 8

Shoreditch Empanada. *At the entrance of San Pedro Market there is a stall that sells the most delicious Andina empanadas. They are mostly filled using offcuts of meat, but I wanted this recipe to be veggie, as many of our Andina customers, who live and work in Shoreditch prefer it that way.*

6 waxy, salad potatoes, peeled and cut into 5mm cubes

2 tbsp olive oil

1 small onion, finely chopped

6 large leaves of Swiss chard with stems, leaves finely shredded, stems reserved

4 spring onions, finely sliced

1 amarillo or red medium-heat chilli, deseeded and finely chopped

¼ tsp ground cumin

1 egg, beaten, for egg wash

1 tsp icing sugar, to serve

Salt and freshly ground black pepper

For the pastry

250g plain flour, plus extra for rolling

1 tsp icing sugar

½ tsp baking powder

20g butter, cubed and chilled

First, make the pastry. Sift the flour, icing sugar and baking powder into a bowl and add ½ teaspoon of salt. Rub in the butter until the mixture resembles fine breadcrumbs, then gradually incorporate 250ml of water until you have a stiff dough. (You can do this in a food processor or stand mixer, if you prefer.) Tip out the dough onto a lightly floured surface and knead gently until smooth, then wrap the dough in clingfilm and allow to rest in the fridge for at least 1 hour.

Meanwhile, make the filling. Put the potato in a saucepan and cover with water. Salt the water, then bring to the boil over a high heat. Reduce the heat to low and simmer for about 4–5 minutes until the potatoes are tender. Drain and set aside.

Heat the olive oil in a large frying pan over a low heat. Add the onion and sauté for about 10 minutes until the onione is starting to soften, then add the Swiss chard stems. Cook for a further 3–4 minutes, then add the shredded Swiss chard leaves, the spring onion, chilli and cooked potato. Sprinkle in the cumin and season with salt and pepper. Set aside to cool.

Preheat the oven to 180°C (gas mark 4). Remove the pastry from the fridge and divide it into 16 equal pieces. On a lightly floured surface, roll each piece into a round of about 12cm in diameter. Place a large spoonful (about 50g) of the potato mixture in the centre of 8 rounds, then brush the exposed edges with egg wash and place another pastry round on top. Mould the top layer of pastry around the filling, then crimp the edges. Brush with more egg wash. Bake the empanadas in the oven for about 25 minutes until golden brown. Dust with icing sugar before serving hot or cold.

Conejo al Palo

SERVES 4

Whole Roast Rabbit on a Stick. *Drive northwards out of Cusco, pass through the famous market town of Pisac and head towards the beautiful Urubamba Valley. There are many places to eat along the way, but the town of Lamay is the most interesting, as that's where you can find barbecue guinea pig on a stick. In this recipe I'm using rabbit, as the flavour is just as delicious, and the meat is similar but more accessible.*

1 rabbit, cleaned, left whole

A few rosemary sprigs

2 barbecued corn-on-the-cobs, halved, to serve

2 sweet potatoes, baked, to serve

3 tbsp huacatay herb paste (see p.132), to serve

Salt and freshly ground black pepper

For the marinade

50ml olive oil

100ml white wine vinegar

2 tbsp garlic purée

1 tsp dried thyme

1 tsp dried oregano

½ tsp ground cumin

On the day before you intend to cook, mix all the marinade ingredients together in a large bowl (big enough to hold the rabbit) and season with plenty of salt and pepper. Add the rabbit, massaging the marinade into the flesh. Cover (or put the whole thing, including the marinade, into a large, sealable plastic bag) and marinate in the fridge overnight.

Remove the rabbit from the fridge 1 hour before you want to cook it, to bring it up to room temperature, and stuff the cavity with rosemary. Reserve the marinade.

To cook, you have three options:

You can cook the rabbit on a spit over a hot charcoal grill or barbecue. In this case, spear the rabbit on a long wooden stick and suspend it about 20cm over the coals. Cook for about 30 minutes, turning and using a pastry brush to baste with the marinade at least every 15 minutes throughout, until the rabbit is cooked through and a combination of lightly browned and slightly charred in places.

To barbecue the rabbit without the spit, place the rabbit on the grill and cook slowly for about 1 hour, turning and basting as before.

To oven roast, preheat the oven to 200°C (gas mark 6). Place the rabbit on a rack over a roasting tin and roast for 1 hour, basting every 15 minutes, until cooked through.

Serve the rabbit whole for everyone to help themselves, with barbecued corn cobs, halved baked sweet potatoes and a drizzle of huacatay paste.

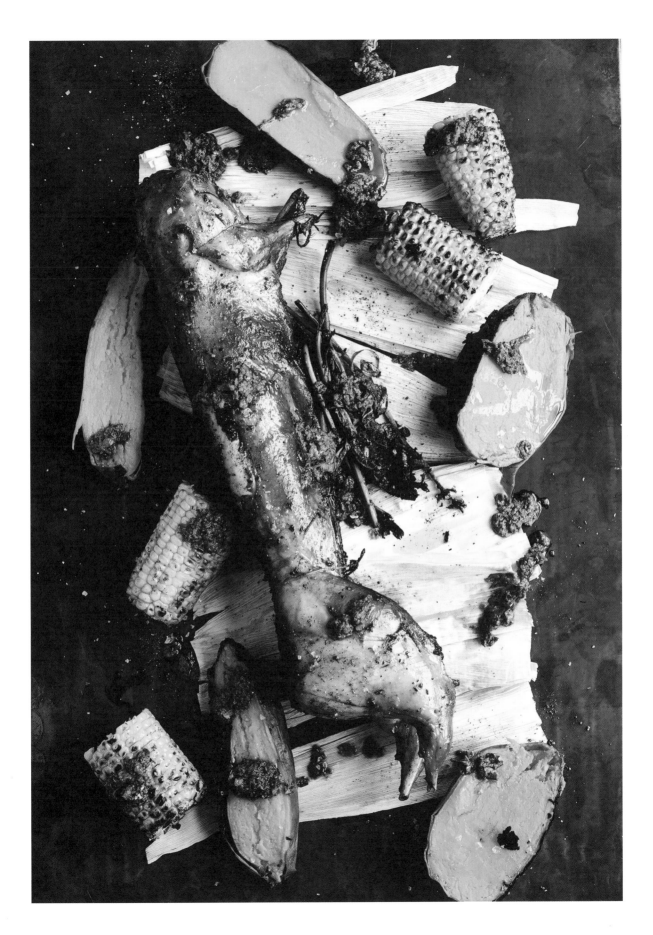

Coliflor a la Brasa

SERVES 4

Charred Cauliflower. *Cauliflower can take on so many flavours when charred. Here, a nutty crust, a sweetish middle and a flicker of bitter scents, all smothered in a creamy herb sauce, make for a perfect starter or side dish.*

1 small cauliflower, broken into florets

2 tbsp olive oil, for grilling

3 tbsp raw peanuts

For the huacatay herb paste (makes about 100g)

A large bunch of huacatay herb; or a small bunch each of coriander, tarragon, mint and parsley

20ml red wine vinegar

Salt

For the uchucuta sauce (makes about 300ml)

2 tbsp olive oil

½ red onion, finely chopped

4 garlic cloves, crushed

4 medium-heat red chillies, finely chopped

125g baby spinach leaves, blanched

20g queso fresco or feta, crumbled

50ml huacatay paste (see above)

1 large ripe beef tomato, finely chopped

Put the cauliflower florets in a steamer and steam for about 8 minutes until just al dente, then plunge the florets into a bowl of iced water to stop them from cooking. Allow the cauliflower to cool for 5 minutes, then drain. Alternatively, put the cauliflower into a colander and set under running cold water until it has cooled down completely.

Make the huacatay paste. Put all the ingredients in a food processor or blender with 10ml of water. Blitz until you have a smooth paste. Add a splash more water to loosen, if necessary. Season with salt to taste. Set aside.

Make the uchucuta sauce. Heat the olive oil in a small frying pan over a medium heat. Add the onion, garlic and chilli and sauté for about 8–10 minutes until the onion has softened and the garlic is soft but not browned. Tip the contents of the pan into a food processor or blender and add the spinach, cheese and huacatay paste. Blitz until coarse, then stir in the tomato and set aside.

Heat a large griddle pan until it is too hot to hold your hand over. Drizzle the olive oil over the cauliflower and toss the florets briefly so that they are evenly covered. Put the florets on the griddle and cook for 5–6 minutes, turning regularly, until they are all charred in places. (You can also do this on a barbecue.)

Toast the peanuts in a dry frying pan for 1–2 minutes until lightly coloured, then tip them into a mortar and use a pestle to crush coarsely.

Serve the cauliflower in a bowl sprinkled with the crushed toasted peanuts, with the uchucuta sauce on the side.

Vegetarian, Gluten-free

Espárragos a la Parrilla

SERVES 4

Grilled Asparagus with Huancayo Sauce. *When asparagus is in season, grilling is one of the most delicious ways to cook it – the charred flavours marry so well with Huancayo sauce. As you're grilling, try not to let the nibs of the spears burn too much, and keep the whole asparagus al dente.*

500g asparagus, woody stems snapped off

2 tbsp olive oil

1 tbsp cancha corn, roughly crushed, to serve

1 quantity of Huancayo sauce (see p.51), to serve

Heat a griddle until it is too hot to hold your hand over. Wash the asparagus well, shake off the excess water, then drizzle with the olive oil. Place the asparagus spears on the griddle for 5–6 minutes, turning regularly, until just al dente and marked with deep char lines from the griddle. (You can also do this on a barbecue.)

Serve the asparagus sprinkled with the crushed cancha corn and with the sauce poured over the top.

Guisos

STEWS

Sango con Adobo de Pato

SERVES 4

Freekeh Mash with Panca Duck. *Once commonly eaten in the southern Andes, sango is an ancient dish now often replaced with rice. It's sweet and hearty, which makes it suitable as a dessert, but it's also great with any rich, savoury stew. Here, I've paired it with stewed duck in a recipe that has its origins in the northern Andes.*

4 duck legs, pricked all over

1 tbsp olive oil

2 onions, finely chopped or grated

50g panca chilli paste (see p.20)

1 tsp dried oregano

6 dried bay leaves

100ml chicha (see p.199) or dry cider

500ml chicken stock

Salt and freshly ground black pepper

For the marinade

100ml freshly squeezed orange juice

4 garlic cloves, crushed

1 tsp ground cumin

For the sango

100g freekeh

50g butter

50g plain flour

50g yacon syrup or light soft brown sugar

250ml full-fat milk

50g queso fresco or feta, crumbled

1 tbsp raw peanuts, roughly chopped, to decorate

1 tbsp raisins, soaked in a little hot water and drained, to decorate

First, put all the marinade ingredients in a large bowl, whisk together and season with plenty of salt. Add the duck legs to the marinade. Cover and marinate in the fridge for 2 hours.

Heat the olive oil in a large, deep-sided frying pan or casserole. Remove the duck legs from the marinade and pat dry, reserving the marinade. Sear the duck legs until the skin is a deep golden brown all over and much of the fat has rendered out, about 3–4 minutes on each side. Remove the duck from the pan and set aside. Strain off the fat from the pan and add the onion. Fry for 7–8 minutes until lightly coloured and softened, then add the chilli paste, oregano, bay leaves, chicha or cider, and chicken stock. Season, return the duck to the pan, reduce the heat and simmer for 1–1½ hours until the duck is cooked and tender.

Meanwhile, make the sango. Rinse the freekeh thoroughly, then put it in a saucepan and toast it over a medium heat for about 3–4 minutes until aromatic. Pour in 200ml of water, bring to the boil and season with salt. Reduce the heat to very low, cover and simmer until the freekeh is cooked and the water has been absorbed (about 20 minutes). In a separate saucepan, melt the butter over a medium heat, then stir in the flour to create a paste. Continue to cook until the flour has had a chance to cook out (this removes the flour's raw flavour), about 3–4 minutes, then add the syrup or sugar and the milk. Reduce the heat and whisk until the sugar (if using) has dissolved and the sauce is smooth. Tip in the cooked freekeh and the cheese. Season with a little salt and pepper, then cook gently for about 10 minutes, stirring continuously, until the sauce has thickened and the cheese has melted. Remove from the heat and keep warm.

When the duck is ready, remove it from its cooking liquor and keep warm. Boil the contents of the pan for about 5 minutes until the liquid has reduced to a syrupy sauce. To serve, divide the sango between 4 plates. Top with the duck and drizzle over some sauce. Decorate with a sprinkling of peanuts and raisins.

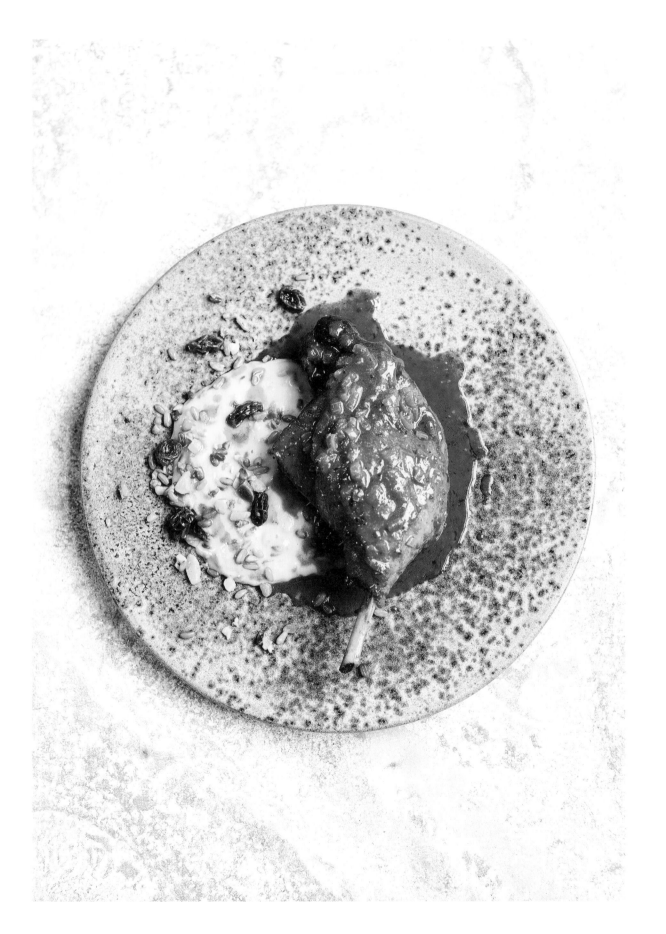

Locro de Zapallo

SERVES 4

Pumpkin Casserole. *My Great Aunt Otilia used to make this locro at her house in Lima. It's an Andina dish by origin, but it has variations using different meats all over South America. This straightforward and quick version is my favourite. I like it served with white quinoa, but you could use white rice, if you prefer.*

2 tbsp olive oil

1 onion, finely chopped

1 garlic clove, finely chopped

1 tbsp amarillo chilli paste
(see p.20)

½ tsp dried oregano

500g pumpkin or butternut squash,
peeled and cut into 4cm cubes

1 large potato, peeled and cut
into 2.5cm cubes

250ml vegetable stock

50g broad beans

50g choclo corn kernels or
sweetcorn kernels

50g peas

100ml single cream
or evaporated milk

50g white quinoa, cooked
(see p. 64)

100g queso fresco or feta,
roughly broken

Chopped flat-leaf parsley, to serve

Salt and freshly ground black pepper

Heat the olive oil in a large saucepan or casserole over a low heat. Add the onion and sauté for about 10 minutes until soft, then add the garlic, chilli paste and oregano and stir for a further 2–3 minutes until the garlic has softened slightly and everything is well combined.

Add the butternut squash and the potato, then cover with the vegetable stock and bring the liquid to the boil, then reduce the heat, cover and simmer for 15 minutes until the butternut squash and potato are just tender and the liquid has reduced a little. Add the broad beans, the choclo or sweetcorn, and the peas, cover again and simmer for 5 minutes more until the broad beans are just tender. Add the single cream or evaporated milk and stir to combine. Cook for a further 1–2 minutes, uncovered, to heat through. Season with salt and pepper.

Serve the stew in shallow bowls with the quinoa and the cheese on the side, and sprinkled with a little chopped parsley.

Guiso de Cabrito de Santiago

SERVES 4–6

Santiago Kid Goat Stew. *In Santiago, which was my grandmother's nearest town, they love to eat the whole kid goat, letting nothing go to waste. Using every piece of the animal, the meat is stewed slowly, to ensure you get the very best flavour. In the spirit of that tradition, when you make this stew, don't let anything go to waste – eat any leftovers the following day, or freeze them for another time.*

600g goat meat, diced

2 tbsp olive oil

1 red onion, finely chopped

3 garlic cloves, crushed

50g coriander, blended with a little water to make a paste

100g pumpkin flesh, diced

250ml chicha (see p.199) or dry cider

250ml lamb stock

½ cassava, peeled and cut into chunks

For the marinade

1 tbsp white wine vinegar

1 tsp panca chilli paste (see p.20)

2 garlic cloves, crushed

½ tsp ground cumin

½ tsp dried oregano

¼ tsp ground black pepper

1 tsp salt

For the beans

1 tbsp olive oil

1 onion, finely chopped

3 garlic cloves, crushed

2 tsp amarillo chilli paste (see p.20)

2 tins of cooked cannellini beans, drained (about 500g drained weight)

First, make the marinade by mixing all the marinade ingredients together in a large bowl.

Put the diced goat meat in the bowl with the marinade and rub in thoroughly. Cover and marinate in the fridge for at least 3 hours.

When the goat meat is ready, heat 1 tablespoon of the olive oil in a large casserole over a high heat. Add the meat and cook until well browned on all sides. Remove with a slotted spoon and set aside. Add the remaining olive oil, then reduce the heat to medium, add the red onion and sauté for about 10 minutes until softened. Add the garlic and cook for 2–3 minutes more, then add about two-thirds of the coriander paste and return the goat to the casserole. Add the pumpkin, stir to coat and then pour in the chicha or cider and the lamb stock. Bring the liquid to the boil, then reduce the heat to low and cover. Cook for about 45 minutes, or until the meat is tender.

Meanwhile, make the beans. Heat the olive oil in a saucepan over a medium heat. Add the onion and sauté until softened, then add the garlic and chilli paste and cook for 1–2 minutes more. Add the beans and stir to combine, then remove from the heat and keep warm.

Bring a pan of salted water to the boil over a medium heat and add the chunks of cassava. Boil for 20–25 minutes until tender.

To assemble the dish, stir the remaining coriander paste into the goat stew, then serve on plates with the beans and the cassava on the side.

Adobo Ayacuchano

SERVES 4

Pork Chops Ayacucho-style. *Originally a way to preserve meats, adobo sauces have, over time, become flavourings for slow-cooked stews. Although this dish is mostly eaten as a weekend breakfast in the Andes, I prefer it for lunch or dinner. If you stew chillies slowly, the heat disappears, leaving just their aromatic footprint. I'm serving this recipe with rice, but sango (see p.138) or sweet potato mash are delicious, too.*

4 pork chops

2 tbsp olive oil

1 cinnamon stick

2 cloves

1 dried bay leaf

Cooked white rice, to serve

Salt and freshly ground black pepper

For the marinade

2 small red onions, cut into wedges

2 tbsp garlic purée

1 tbsp amarillo chilli paste (see p.20)

100g panca chilli paste (see p.20)

2 tsp red wine vinegar

200ml chicha (see p.199) or dry cider

1 tsp dried oregano

½ tsp ground cumin

First, make the marinade. Put all the marinade ingredients in a large bowl with plenty of salt and pepper. Add the pork chops, cover and marinate in the fridge overnight.

Remove the pork chops from the fridge at least 30 minutes before you want to cook them to bring them up to room temperature. When you are ready to cook, heat the oil in a large frying pan over a high heat. Remove the chops from the marinade (but don't discard it), pat them dry with kitchen paper and cook for 2 minutes on each side until they are well seared. Then, pour in the marinade, along with the cinnamon stick, cloves and bay leaf, and season with salt and pepper.

Bring the liquid to the boil, then reduce the heat to low and cover the pan. Leave the chops to braise, very gently, until the meat is tender (about 1 hour). Keep an eye on the sauce as the chops cook and add a splash of water if it looks as though it's becoming too dry.

Serve the pork chops with the sauce and mounds of white, fluffy rice.

Pesque de Quinua

SERVES 4

Quinoa & Cheese Pudding. *I'd long heard about this dish, but I didn't try it until I visited the fabulous Huancahuasi Restaurant in Huancayo recently. Local chef Dave Zavala recommended the dish, and then suggested topping it with cheese. It's quinotto-style (like a risotto but with quinoa), only creamier and more indulgent. You can eat it just as it is, or as a side for a stew, such as Picante de Lengua (see p.146).*

4 tbsp olive oil

1 large onion, very finely chopped or grated

4 garlic cloves, crushed

½ tsp ground cumin

100g white quinoa, cooked (see p.64)

200ml single cream or evaporated milk

200g queso fresco or feta, cubed

100g Cheddar cheese, grated

A handful of mint leaves, finely chopped

Salt and freshly ground black pepper

Heat the olive oil in a large saucepan over a medium heat. Add the onion and sauté for about 10 minutes until softened and lightly golden. Add the garlic and cumin and cook for 2–3 minutes more until the garlic has softened but not browned.

Add the quinoa and the cream or evaporated milk to the pan. Stir to combine and season with salt and pepper. Reduce the heat to low and simmer very gently for about 5 minutes, then add the queso fresco or feta, folding it through the quinoa mixture. When the cheese has warmed through, remove the pan from the heat.

Preheat your grill to its highest setting.

Transfer the quinoa mixture to a large ovenproof dish, or divide it between 4 individual serving dishes and sprinkle the Cheddar over. Put the dish or small dishes under the preheated grill for about 5–7 minutes until the cheese turns golden brown and is bubbling. Sprinkle with the chopped mint and serve immediately.

Picante de Lengua

SERVES 4–6

Puno-style Ox Tongue Stew. *When we first opened Andina many of my team told me 'They will never like it', 'No-one eats tongue in London', 'It's too traditional.' Like a red rag to a bull, that set me on a mission. Four weeks later this humble and supposedly unloved dish was kissing most of our customers' lips with gusto. And smiles followed.*

1 ox tongue

2 tbsp achiote oil
(see below)

2 onions, finely chopped

2 celery sticks, finely chopped

1 large carrot, peeled and diced

2 garlic cloves, finely chopped

100g panca chilli paste (see p.20)

50g amarillo chilli paste (see p.20)

1.25l beef stock, plus extra for
cooking, if necessary

2 tbsp sherry vinegar

1 quantity of Pesque de Quinua
(see p.144), to serve

Salt and freshly ground black pepper

For the achiote oil

1 tbsp achiote or annatto seeds

100ml groundnut or vegetable oil

First, make the achiote oil. Put the seeds and the oil in a small saucepan. Heat gently, swirling the contents of the saucepan regularly, for about 5 minutes until the oil has taken on a deep ochre colour from the seeds. Remove from the heat and strain the oil into a sterilized airtight jar. Allow the oil to cool in the jar, replace the lid and store in the fridge for up to 6 weeks.

To make the dish, put 1 tablespoon of salt in a large bowl of water and add the tongue. Leave to soak for 5–6 hours.

When you are ready to cook, heat the 2 tablespoons of achiote oil in a large saucepan or casserole over a medium heat. Add the onion, celery and carrot and sauté for 6–8 minutes until the onion is soft and everything is starting to brown slightly. Add the garlic and chilli pastes and cook, stirring, for a further 2–3 minutes until the garlic has softened slightly.

Remove the tongue from its soaking water and rinse thoroughly, then add it to the pan with the onion mixture. Pour over the stock – it should just be enough to cover the tongue – and add the sherry vinegar. Season with salt and pepper, then bring the liquid to the boil. As soon as the liquid begins to boil, reduce the heat to low and simmer, covered, for 2½–3 hours until the tongue is very tender. Top up the liquid with more water or stock as it cooks, if necessary – you want the tongue submerged throughout.

When the tongue is ready, remove it from the liquid using a slotted spoon. Leave the tongue to rest until it is cool enough to handle, then peel off the skin and cut or pull out the gristly part at the back. Cut the flesh into thick slices and return them to the stew. Cook for a further 5 minutes until the meat is warmed through, then serve immediately with the Pesque de Quinua on the side.

Picante de Tarwi

SERVES 4

Amantani's Lupin Bean Stew. *I created this dish to pay homage to Amantani, the Cusco-based children's charity of which I am proud to be a part. The recipe is based on a traditional dish originating mainly from Cusco. If you can't find lupin beans you can use butter, cannellini or haricot beans instead.*

650g cooked lupin beans or any large white beans

60ml single cream or evaporated milk

4 potatoes, peeled and cut into 2cm cubes

3 tbsp olive oil

1 large red onion, finely chopped

3 garlic cloves, crushed

1 tbsp amarillo chilli paste (see p.20)

½ tsp ground cumin

¼ tsp ground turmeric

50g queso fresco or feta, crumbled, to serve

A few parsley leaves and a few mint leaves, finely chopped, to serve

Salt and freshly ground black pepper

Put half the beans in a food processor or blender with the cream or evaporated milk and 40ml of water. Blitz until you have a smooth purée.

Bring a saucepan of salted water to the boil over a high heat. Add the potato cubes and cook for 3–4 minutes until just tender.

Heat the olive oil in a large, deep-sided frying pan over a medium heat. Add the red onion and sauté for 7–8 minutes until softened, then add the garlic, the chilli paste and the spices and stir to combine. Add the bean purée, the remaining whole beans and the cooked potatoes to the pan along with 100ml of water and season with salt and pepper. Reduce the heat to low and cook for about 10 minutes, stirring continuously, until heated through.

Serve the stew in bowls sprinkled with the crumbled cheese and the chopped herbs.

Cordero Chukulati

SERVES 4

Slow-and-Low Lamb Shanks & Chocolate. *New ideas for dishes at our restaurants always appear as specials before getting a listing on the menu. This recipe was an instant hit. The magic of the velvety and dark chocolate combined with the succulent lamb shanks and spices makes this dish perfect for autumn.*

2 tbsp olive oil, plus extra for roasting

1 red onion, finely chopped

1 celery stick, finely chopped

1 carrot, finely chopped

1 panca chilli, deseeded and roughly chopped, or 1 tbsp panca chilli paste (see p.20)

2 garlic cloves, finely chopped

200ml red wine

300ml lamb or beef stock

½ bunch of coriander, finely chopped

1 star anise

4 small lamb shanks (about 200g each on the bone)

1 large squash, bulbous part sliced into 4 rounds

15g dark chocolate (at least 70% cocoa solids)

2 dried chestnuts, crumbled, to serve

Salt and freshly ground black pepper

Heat the olive oil in a large casserole over a medium heat. Reduce the heat to low and add the red onion, celery, carrot, chilli or chilli paste and garlic and sauté for about 10 minutes until the onion has softened. Add the red wine, lamb or beef stock and coriander, increase the heat and bring to the boil. Boil for 2 minutes to cook out the wine a little, then season with salt and pepper.

Add the star anise, then the lamb shanks to the pan and reduce the heat to low so that the liquid is very gently simmering. Cover the pan and cook for about 1½ hours, turning the shanks over regularly so that they cook evenly, until the meat is very tender.

Meanwhile, sprinkle the squash discs with a little salt and olive oil and roast in a preheated oven (180°C/gas mark 4) for 30 minutes, or until golden and tender. Keep warm.

Remove the shanks from the casserole and set aside to keep warm. Discard the star anise, then simmer the sauce, uncovered, for about 5 minutes until well reduced to a syrupy consistency, then stir in the chocolate. When the chocolate has melted, remove the casserole from the heat and use a stick blender to blitz the sauce a little, leaving it with plenty of texture.

To serve, put 1 shank on each of 4 dinner plates. Pour equal amounts of the sauce over each shank and sprinkle with the crumbled chestnuts. Serve with a roasted squash disc on the side.

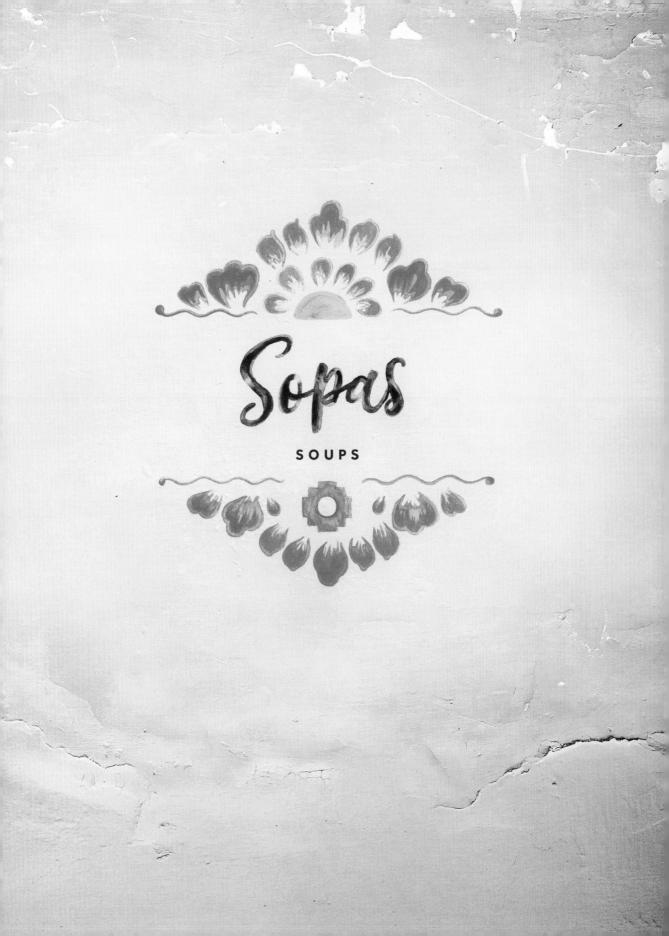

Sopas

SOUPS

Kapchi de Setas

SERVES 4–6

Mushroom & Broad Bean Soup. *This is a seasonal dish that is particularly popular in the regions of Apurímac and Cusco. There, the rainy season gives birth to forest floors covered in flowers among which grow the juiciest and tastiest mushrooms. Use the widest variety of edible seasonal mushrooms you can get hold of to increase the depth of flavour and texture in this dish.*

12 new potatoes, halved lengthways

200g broad beans

4 tbsp olive oil

1 large onion, finely chopped

3 garlic cloves, finely chopped

1 tbsp panca chilli paste (see p.20)

8 large portobello mushrooms (about 800g) or wild equivalent

250ml full-fat milk

1 tbsp huacatay or a few leaves each of coriander, tarragon and parsley, finely chopped

A few mint leaves, finely chopped

100g queso fresco or feta, crumbled

A few micro herbs, to serve

Salt

Put the new potatoes in a saucepan and cover with water. Salt the water, then put the pan over a high heat and bring to the boil. Reduce the heat to low and simmer for 8–10 minutes until just tender. Drain the potatoes and set aside.

Bring a small saucepan of water to the boil over a high heat. Add the broad beans and blanch for 2 minutes, then drain. If the broad beans are particularly large, you may want to peel off the bitter, outer skins (if they are small and tender, there's no need to do this). Set aside.

Heat 1 tablespoon of the olive oil in a large, deep-sided frying pan or casserole. Add the onion and sauté over a medium heat for 10 minutes until soft and translucent. Add the garlic and chilli paste and cook for a further 2–3 minutes until the chilli paste starts to separate. Set aside.

Heat the remaining oil in a large frying pan. Add the mushrooms with a generous pinch of salt and sauté over a medium heat for 5–6 minutes until any liquid they release has evaporated and the mushrooms are softened and glossy. You may have to do this in more than one batch – if so, use the olive oil accordingly.

Add the potatoes and broad beans to the onion mixture, then add the milk. Put the pan or casserole back over a medium heat and simmer for 10 minutes until everything is heated through. Add the huacatay or herb mixture and the mint, then the cooked mushrooms and finally the cheese. Stir everything together and simmer for 4–5 minutes more until the cheese is slightly softened. Serve immediately in bowls sprinkled with the micro herbs.

Caldo Verde de Cajamarca

SERVES 4–6

Cajamarca's Green Soup. *I drove over bumpy dirt roads, through torrential rain and along steep precipices for eight hours to try this soup in the historic city of Cajamarca. Although it is traditionally made with paico and ruda herbs, which are native to the Peruvian Andes, you can use parsley and pak choi. The egg and cheese provide protein, making it a filling main course.*

2 tbsp olive oil

1 large white onion, finely chopped

3 garlic cloves, finely chopped

A large bunch of paico leaves; or a small bunch of parsley and a small bunch of mint

A small bunch of huacatay; or a small bunch of coriander and a few tarragon sprigs

½ head of a small green cabbage or 4 heads of pak choi (about 150g altogether)

4 potatoes, peeled and thickly sliced

4–6 eggs, separated

200g queso fresco or feta, crumbled

Salt and freshly ground black pepper

Heat the olive oil in a large saucepan or casserole. Add the onion and sauté over a medium heat for 10 minutes until soft and translucent. Add the garlic and cook for a further 1–2 minutes to soften.

Meanwhile, put all the herbs in a blender with a little water and blitz to a smooth paste.

When the onion and garlic are ready, add half the herb paste to the pan with the onion mixture, along with the cabbage or pak choi and the potatoes. Stir to combine, then pour in 1.5 litres of water and season well with salt and pepper.

Bring the soup to the boil, then reduce the heat to low and simmer for 25 minutes until the potatoes are very tender. Remove the casserole from the heat and spoon off 2 ladlefuls of stock into a small saucepan over a low heat. Whisk up the egg whites a little and swirl into the casserole of hot soup, then stir in the remaining herb paste and keep warm. Carefully drop the egg yolks into the small saucepan of broth and allow them to poach gently for 2 minutes until warmed through but still runny. Serve up the soup in individual bowls, carefully adding a poached yolk to each bowl (1 yolk per person) and sprinkle with the crumbled cheese.

Note: If it feels too fussy to separate and poach the yolks in this way, you can omit the steps of adding the whites and separating off some stock and instead crack whole eggs into the soup, poaching them directly in the casserole. Serve up 1 whole egg per person.

Vegetarian, Gluten-free

Chupe de Olluco

SERVES 4–6

Olluco Chowder. *The brilliant team at La Tullpa restaurant in Huancayo showed me how to put together this delicious recipe. It's super-easy and quick to make, is great as a starter or a main course, and if you can get your hands on olluco tubers, their distinct flavour will make all the difference.*

2 tbsp olive oil

1 onion, finely chopped

4 garlic cloves, crushed

600g olluco or parsnips, peeled and cut into 2cm cubes

400g floury potatoes (such as Maris Piper), peeled and cut into thin chips

1 tbsp each of finely chopped coriander, parsley, mint and tarragon

100ml full-fat milk

100ml single cream or evaporated milk

1.2l vegetable stock or water

100g broad beans

50g peas

¼ tsp dried oregano

4–6 eggs (1 egg per person)

50g queso fresco or feta, crumbled

Salt and freshly ground black pepper

Heat the olive oil in a large saucepan or casserole. Add the onion and sauté over a medium heat for 10–12 minutes until softened and light golden brown in colour. Add the garlic and cook for a further 2–3 minutes to soften.

Add the olluco or parsnips and the potatoes. Stir to coat in the onion and garlic mixture, then stir in the finely chopped herbs. Season with plenty of salt and pepper, then add the milk and cream or evaporated milk. Add the stock or water and bring to the boil. Reduce the heat to low and simmer for 10 minutes until the olluco and potatoes are tender but not collapsing.

Add the broad beans and peas, along with the oregano. Stir the chowder so that it starts to swirl. Quickly crack in the eggs, one at a time, so that each egg poaches in the liquid. Simmer until the whites are set and the yolks are still soft. (Alternatively, you can poach the eggs separately and add them to the chowder at the last minute.)

Sprinkle in the crumbled cheese and serve piping hot, making sure that each person gets an egg.

Patasca de Feli

SERVES 6–8

Feli's Hominy & Tripe Soup. *Patasca is served in many regions of the Andes, each region adding its own local chillies, hominy or offal. The region of Huancavelica, where my Aunt Feli comes from, makes some of the most delicious versions of all, so I named this recipe in her honour.*

200g mote or barley, soaked overnight, then drained, simmered in fresh water for 3 hours, and drained again

350g tripe, cleaned, thoroughly rinsed and cut into 1.5cm strips

2 tbsp olive oil

1 large red onion, finely chopped

3 garlic cloves, crushed

½ tbsp panca chilli paste (see p.20)

400g pork, on the bone, cut into 4 pieces, or 4 pork shanks

2 large pieces of oxtail

200g chuño or carapulcra dried potatoes (rinsed, soaked and drained; see p.128); or 400g new potatoes, peeled and quartered

A small bunch of parsley, roughly chopped

2 spring onions, finely chopped, to serve

Salt and freshly ground black pepper

If using mote, put it in a saucepan, cover with water and bring to the boil over a high heat. Cook fiercely for 10 minutes, then drain and set aside.

Put the tripe in a saucepan and cover completely with cold water. Add 1 tablespoon of salt and bring the salted water to the boil over a high heat, then reduce the heat to low and simmer for 15 minutes. Drain and rinse thoroughly. If the tripe still smells of ammonia, repeat this process once more, then set aside.

Heat the olive oil in a large saucepan or casserole. Add the onion and sauté over a low heat for 10 minutes until softened. Add the garlic and chilli paste and continue to cook for 2–3 minutes until the garlic has started to soften.

Add the tripe, pork and oxtail to the pan with the onion and chilli mixture and cover with water. Bring to the boil over a high heat, then reduce the heat to low. Allow to simmer but keep an eye on it, skimming off any mushroom-coloured foam that may collect at the top. Continue to simmer, skimming the foam, until the foam turns white (about 5 minutes).

Add the drained mote or barley and season with salt and pepper. Cover the pan, then cook very gently for about 1½–2 hours. Add the soaked dried or raw new potatoes and continue to cook for a further 15–20 minutes until the potatoes are just tender. Season with salt to taste.

Remove the pan from the heat and adjust the seasoning, if necessary. Stir in the parsley just before serving, then serve in bowls with a sprinkling of chopped spring onion.

Huallpa Chupe

SERVES 4

Amarillo Chilli Chicken Soup. *Classic chicken broth used to be my most comforting recovery meal when I feel poorly. Until, that is, I tried this soup in the province of Huancayo. It's warming without being heavy and comes with added pick-me-up and aromas from the amarillo chilli.*

2 tbsp olive oil

2 large onions, finely chopped or grated

2 yellow peppers, deseeded and very finely chopped or grated

6 garlic cloves, crushed

100g amarillo chilli paste (see p.20)

1 tsp ground cumin

4 chicken breasts, skin on

1.2l chicken stock

2 large potatoes, peeled and cut into 5cm chunks

1 red pepper, deseeded and cut into large chunks

50g white rice

50g peas

50g broad beans

50g sweetcorn kernels

A small bunch of parsley, chopped, to serve

Salt and freshly ground black pepper

Heat the olive oil in a large casserole. Add the onion and yellow pepper, and sauté over a fairly high heat for 5–6 minutes until they start to soften and colour. Add the garlic, chilli paste and cumin and stir for 2–3 minutes until the chilli paste starts to separate.

Add the chicken, skin-side down and cook over a high heat for 5–6 minutes until the skin is lightly browned. Turn over the breasts and pour in the stock, then add the potato, red pepper and rice. Season with salt and pepper.

Bring the stock to the boil, then reduce the heat and simmer gently until the chicken is cooked through and the rice is cooked (about 20 minutes). Add the peas, broad beans and sweetcorn and simmer for 3–4 minutes to warm through.

Serve ladled into individual serving bowls, with 1 chicken breast per serving, and sprinkled with plenty of chopped parsley.

Note: For true nose-to-tail eating, you can also use a whole chicken for this dish. Cut the chicken into pieces (legs, thighs, wings, breasts), cooking everything as above. This time, though, add the carcass to the pot, too. When everything is cooked, remove the carcass to a plate. Pick off every piece of meat you can find on the carcass and reintroduce the meat to the soup. Discard the carcass bones and serve the soup as before.

Chupe de Camarones Antiguo

SERVES 4

Ancient Prawn Chowder. *The warm and loving welcome I received from chef Mónica Huerta Alpaca at her Picantería La Nueva Palomino in Arequipa was matched only by her heavenly version of this classic Andina dish, handed down through five generations of her family. Local river prawns have greater intensity of flavour than ocean prawns, but of course you can use whichever is available.*

2 tbsp olive oil

1 red onion, finely chopped

5 large garlic cloves, crushed

1 tbsp panca chilli paste (see p.20)

2 tbsp amarillo chilli paste
(see p.20)

2 tsp tomato purée

½ tsp ground cumin

½ tsp dried oregano

100g uncooked mixed quinoa

1 choclo corn or corn-on-the-cob,
cut into chunks

1 large potato, peeled but left whole

600g large raw prawns, 4 left intact,
the rest peeled, heads removed
and deveined (keep the shells and
heads to make the stock)

4 eggs (1 egg per person)

100g peas

100ml single cream or
evaporated milk

50g queso fresco or feta, crumbled

Salt and freshly ground black pepper

For the shellfish stock

1 tbsp olive oil

Discarded heads and shells from
the prawns (see above)

1.5l fish stock or water

First, make the shellfish stock. Heat the olive oil in a large saucepan and add the prawn heads and shells. Stir over a high heat for 3–4 minutes until bright pink and smelling very aromatic, then pour over the fish stock or water. Reduce the heat to medium and simmer for 5 minutes, then turn down the heat to low and simmer very gently for a further 30 minutes. Use a potato masher to mash the shells and release all their juices. Strain the liquid through a sieve and press down with a metal spoon to release all the stock. Discard the prawn heads and shells.

To make the soup, heat the olive oil in a large saucepan or casserole. Add the red onion and sauté over a low heat for about 10 minutes until softened. Add the garlic, chilli pastes and tomato purée, along with the cumin and oregano. Cook, stirring regularly, for a further 2 minutes until the chilli pastes start to separate.

Pour in the shellfish stock and season with salt and pepper. Add the quinoa, choclo or corn cob, potato and the peeled and unpeeled prawns, and simmer for about 15 minutes until the prawns are pink and cooked through and everything else is almost cooked.

Crack in the eggs and poach them directly in the soup for 3 minutes until the egg whites are set and the yolks are still soft. (Alternatively, you can poach the eggs separately and add them at the last minute.) Season with salt.

Add the peas and evaporated milk or cream and simmer for a further 2 minutes until the peas are tender but still a fresh green colour.

Serve the soup in individual bowls, making sure everyone gets an egg and unpeeled prawn, sprinkled with the cheese.

Caldo de Cabeza

SERVES 6

Lamb's Head & Vegetables Consommé. *This dish is rooted in the traditions of Pasco, Apurímac, Cusco, Huánuco and Arequipa – but my kids and their friends in London love it, too. Any good butcher will cut up the lamb's head for you if you ask, and Halal butchers often have lambs' heads in stock. Use the whole head, including the brains and tongue, which are essential for flavour.*

1 lamb's head, cut into 6 pieces, tongue reserved

2 large onions, roughly chopped

Cloves from ½ head of garlic, sliced

1 tsp ground cumin

1 tsp dried oregano

4 sweet potatoes, peeled and cut into thick chunks

1 red pepper, deseeded and finely diced

200g sweetcorn kernels

100g peas

Salt and freshly ground black pepper

Put the pieces of head, including the tongue (cut this into pieces if you like), in a very large saucepan or stock pot. Cover with water – this will probably take at least 2.5–3 litres. Bring to the boil over a high heat. Leave to boil, skimming off any mushroom-coloured foam that collects on the surface. Stop when the foam turns white (about 4–5 minutes).

Add the onion, garlic, cumin and oregano and season with plenty of salt and pepper. Reduce the heat to low and simmer, partially covered, for at least 2 hours, or until the meat on the head is close to falling off the bone, the tongue is tender and the broth has reduced by more than one-third.

Add the sweet potato and red pepper. Simmer for a further 15 minutes until the vegetables are tender, then add the sweetcorn and peas. Simmer for 3–4 minutes, then taste and adjust the seasoning, if necessary. Serve immediately, leaving the meat on the bone, ladled into deep bowls.

Chochoca

SERVES 6–8

Beef & Corn Soup. *Picanterías serve a particular soup on each day of the week. In Arequipa, chochoca is the soup served on Wednesday. I've never been able to find out why, but the tradition amuses me, as I used to have this soup any day of the week when I lived in Peru. Chochoca is a great starter: its flavour is simple yet powerful. You can make it with a mixture of vegetables and veggie stock instead of meat, if you prefer.*

1kg beef short ribs

1 large onion, sliced

4 garlic cloves, finely chopped

2 tbsp panca chilli paste (see p.20)

2 large floury potatoes (such as Maris Piper), peeled and cut into 4cm cubes

1 choclo corn or corn-on-the-cob, cut into 4 pieces

1 leek, finely diced

2 celery sticks, finely diced

100g semolina

A small bunch of mint, leaves picked, to serve

Salt

Put the beef ribs in a large saucepan or casserole and cover with water. Bring to the boil over a high heat and skim off any mushroom-coloured foam that collects on the surface. When the foam has subsided (about 4–5 minutes), add the onion and garlic, along with plenty of salt. Cover, reduce the heat to low and simmer very gently for 3–4 hours until the meat is falling off the bone.

Remove the ribs from the broth, then pull the meat off the bones and add it back to the broth. Stir in the chilli paste, then add the potatoes, choclo or corn cob pieces, leek and celery. Increase the heat to return to the boil, then lower it again and simmer for a further 25 minutes, until the potatoes are soft. Add the semolina and stir until the soup has thickened.

Serve the soup piping hot in bowls, sprinkled with the mint leaves.

Chairo de Chambi

SERVES 6–8

Chambi's Soup. *In another life I would have loved to have been a photographer. Martín Chambi to be precise. Chambi was born in Puno, and his work from the early 20th century has influenced all Peruvian photographers since. This dish is the most representative from Chambi's place of birth, and I'm sure he ate it regularly – in his honour, I've named my recipe after him.*

2 tbsp olive oil

500g ossobuco (veal shank)

2 thick slices of on-the-bone lamb neck (about 300g altogether)

1 red onion, finely chopped

3 garlic cloves, crushed

2 tbsp amarillo chilli paste (see p.20)

75g beef jerky, soaked in warm water for 1 hour, then drained

1 tsp dried oregano

150g mote or barley, soaked overnight, drained, simmered in fresh water for 3 hours, then drained

125g wheatberries

50g chuño dried potatoes (rinsed, soaked and drained; see p.128); or 100g new potatoes, peeled and quartered

1 large floury potato (such as Maris Piper), peeled and cut into 4cm cubes

1 large carrot, peeled and diced

100g pumpkin, peeled and cut into 4cm cubes

1 choclo corn or corn-on-the-cob, cut into 4 pieces

100g broad beans

¼ head of green cabbage, shredded

A few mint and parsley leaves, finely chopped, to serve

Salt and ground black pepper

Heat the olive oil in a large saucepan or casserole. When very hot, add the ossobuco and lamb neck and sear over a high heat for 5–6 minutes until well browned on all sides. Remove the meat from the casserole and set aside. Add the red onion to the pan or casserole and sauté over a low heat for 10 minutes until softened, then add the garlic, chilli paste and beef jerky and cook for a further 2–3 minutes until the garlic has softened.

Return the meat to the pan and sprinkle over the oregano. Add enough water to just cover the meat. Add the mote or barley, then season with salt and pepper. Bring the liquid to the boil over a high heat, then reduce the heat to low and simmer, partially covered, for 1 hour.

Add the wheatberries, chuño or new potatoes to the pan along with the floury potato, carrot, pumpkin and choclo or corn cob pieces. Increase the heat and bring to the boil once more, then again turn down the heat to low, partially cover the pan, and simmer for at least 1 hour until the meat is falling off the bone and tender, and the vegetables are cooked through. Keep an eye on the soup and add a little more water if it starts to look too thick.

Add the broad beans and cabbage and simmer for a further 2–3 minutes until the cabbage is tender but still a fresh green. Serve the soup in large bowls, dividing the meat evenly between them, and sprinkle with a few chopped mint and parsley leaves.

El Puchero

SERVES 6

Traditional Andina Broth. *This classic recipe is served all over the Andes in homes and from street stalls. Traditionally, it's eaten at carnival time, during February. The slow-cooked broth releases aromas that fill the air to mark the beginning of the festival season.*

2 tbsp olive oil

1 large onion, finely chopped

2 garlic cloves, finely chopped

100g dried chickpeas, soaked overnight and drained

100g piece of beef brisket

100g piece of pork loin

100g piece of lamb neck fillet

100g cecina, bresaola or air-dried ham

1 tsp dried oregano

1 choclo corn or corn-on-the-cob, cut into 6 chunks

1 celery stick, cut into large chunks

2 carrots, peeled and cut into large chunks

1 large potato, peeled

1 cassava or parsnip, peeled and halved

1 sweet potato, peeled and cut into 4–6 thick slices

½ head of a green cabbage, cut into 2 wedges

Salt and freshly ground black pepper

Heat the olive oil in a large casserole. Add the onion and sauté over a high heat for 2 minutes, then reduce the heat to low and add the garlic. Cook for a further 2–3 minutes until the garlic softens.

Pour 1.5 litres of water into the casserole and add the chickpeas. Increase the heat and boil fiercely for 10 minutes, then reduce the heat until the liquid is simmering gently. Add the 3 meat pieces, then watch for a few minutes and skim off any mushroom-coloured foam that collects on the surface of the water. You can stop watching when the foam becomes white (about 4–5 minutes). Half-cover the casserole with a lid and leave the soup to simmer for 30 minutes, then add the cecina (or alternative), oregano, choclo or corn cob, celery, carrot, potato, cassava or parsnip, and sweet potato. Season with salt and pepper, half-cover again and simmer for a further 45 minutes until the vegetables are tender. Then, add the cabbage and cook for 3–4 minutes until the cabbage has wilted down but is still a fresh green colour. Taste the soup and adjust the seasoning, if necessary.

To serve, transfer all of the meat and vegetables to a big serving dish, pour over some of the hot broth and serve in the middle of the table, with the remaining hot broth on the side for everyone to help themselves.

Postres

DESSERTS

Huayno de Chocolate

SERVES 6–8

Chocolate Song. *Great dishes are like great songs: each has ingredients that blend beautifully together to create a masterpiece. Huaynos are one of the most representative musical genres of the Andes and, like the best of them, this dish has harmony and rhythm in its combination of flavours.*

2 ripe avocados, halved, destoned and peeled

100g dark chocolate (at least 70% cocoa solids)

100g yacon syrup or maple syrup

50g cocoa powder

1 tsp vanilla extract

50ml hazelnut milk

A few edible flower petals, to serve

For the tamarillo crème anglaise

150ml full-fat milk

25g sugar

2 egg yolks

1 very ripe tamarillo, peeled and flesh sieved to a purée

For the maíz morado crumble

50g purple corn flour or cocoa powder

25g caster sugar

50g butter

For the plantain chips

1 green plantain or sweet potato, peeled and thinly sliced into strips or rounds

Vegetable oil, for deep frying

1 tsp icing sugar

To make the chocolate avocado mousse, purée the avocado until smooth. Melt the chocolate with the syrup, cocoa powder, vanilla extract and hazelnut milk in a saucepan over a very low heat, stirring and watching it to make sure the chocolate doesn't split. Remove from the heat and allow to cool to body temperature. Stir in the avocado purée, then transfer to a bowl, cover with clingfilm and refrigerate for at least 2 hours to chill.

To make the crème anglaise, heat the milk in a pan over a low heat until just below boiling, then remove from the heat. In a separate bowl, whisk the sugar and egg yolks until pale and mousse-like. Pour the milk into the egg and sugar mixture, whisking as you do so, then return everything to the saucepan. Cook over a very gentle heat, stirring continuously, until the mixture starts to thicken (it's ready when it coats the back of a spoon and you can draw a line through it), about 5–7 minutes. Transfer to a bowl and cover with clingfilm, then allow to cool. When cold, place in the fridge to chill thoroughly, then stir the sieved tamarillo purée through the crème anglaise.

To make the crumble, preheat the oven to 200°C (gas mark 6). Mix the flour and sugar together, then rub in the butter until the mixture resembles sand. Sprinkle this over a baking tray and bake for 20 minutes until crisp. Allow to cool, breaking it up again if it has clumped together – you still want the texture of sand.

To make the plantain or sweet potato chips, half-fill a saucepan with vegetable oil, or use a deep-fat fryer, and heat the oil to about 160°C. Fry the plantain or sweet potato slices until crisp and golden brown in places (about 3–4 minutes). Remove from the oil and set aside to drain on kitchen paper. Dust with icing sugar.

To assemble, sprinkle some of the crumble on a serving plate. Add the mousse, drizzle with the crème anglaise and top with the plantain or sweet potato chips, and a few flower petals, to serve.

Sueño de Lúcuma y Cereza

SERVES 4–6

Lúcuma & Cherry Dream. *Lúcuma is a fruit native to the Andes. Legend has it that a maiden living in the highlands of Peru refused all proposals. One night she dreamt she was sitting under a lúcuma tree when a fruit fell into her lap. She ate it, looked up and fell in love with a bird perched in the branches. When she woke a suitor came to visit her. Recalling her dream she accepted his proposal. The lúcuma dream was born.*

125g lúcuma purée; or 50g lúcuma powder mixed with 100ml water

200ml full-fat milk

2 egg yolks

50g caster sugar

150g white chocolate, broken into squares

200ml whipping cream

A few small mint leaves, to serve

Edible dirt (see p.178), to serve (optional)

For the pisco-infused cherries

200g frozen pitted Morello or black cherries

60g yacon syrup or 100g caster sugar

300ml pisco or whisky

2 pared pieces of orange zest

1 star anise

½ cinnamon stick

For the cherry jam

250g unsweetened cherry purée or frozen black cherries

75g jam sugar

The day before you want to serve the dish, make the pisco-infused cherries. Put all the ingredients in a sterilized glass jar and leave to infuse for 24 hours, turning the jar over regularly, to help the sugar dissolve (if using) and the flavours to develop.

On the day you intend to serve the dish, first make the cherry jam. Put the cherry purée or frozen cherries in a saucepan and add the jam sugar. Cook over a low heat until the sugar has dissolved, then bring to the boil and cook for 5 minutes, stirring continuously, until you reach a jam-like consistency. Set aside.

To make the mousse, put the lúcuma and milk in a saucepan and whisk to combine. Put the pan over a high heat and bring the mixture to the boil, then remove from the heat. In a separate bowl, whisk the egg yolks and sugar together until the mixture is very pale and mousse-like.

Gradually pour the milk and lúcuma mixture into the bowl with the eggs and sugar, stirring continuously. When the mixtures are combined, pour everything back into the saucepan and warm gently over a low heat, still stirring continuously for 10 minutes, until you have a custard. It is ready when the mixture coats the back of a spoon and you can draw a line through it.

Add the white chocolate to the pan with the custard and stir until it has completely melted. Turn off the heat and allow the mixture to cool to body temperature.

Whisk the whipping cream until it forms soft peaks, then fold into the white chocolate custard. Spoon the mousse into individual serving glasses or into one serving bowl or piped onto individual plates. Put in the fridge for at least 4 hours until well chilled and lightly set. Serve with spoonfuls of cherry jam (store any leftover in a jar in the fridge for 1 week) and a few pisco-infused cherries and mint leaves. Sprinkle with edible dirt, if you wish.

Vegetarian, Gluten-free

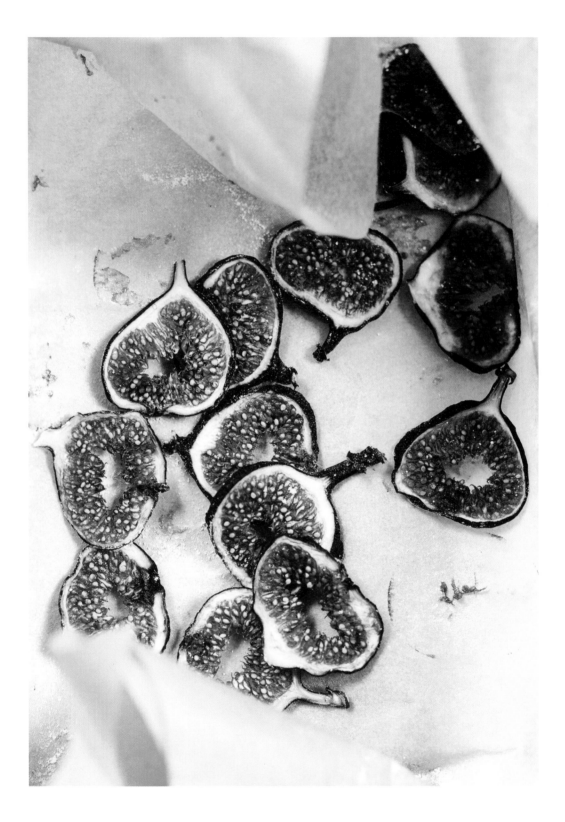

Higos con Crema de Vainilla

SERVES 4

Confit Figs with Vanilla Cream. *For me, figs are the most fascinating and beautiful fruit, and they remind me of the many journeys I've made in the region of La Libertad. This is my absolute favourite dessert from that region. For this dish the riper the figs, the better, so be choosy; if you let them soak in the syrup, the flavours will blend even more intensely.*

8 soft, ready-to-eat figs, plus 2 extra, sliced, to serve

For the confit syrup

100g panela, palm sugar, jaggery or light soft brown sugar

80g yacon syrup or dark brown sugar

2 star anise

1 cinnamon stick

A pared piece of orange zest

2 fig leaves

For the mascarpone vanilla cream

150g mascarpone

125ml whipping cream

25g icing sugar

Seeds scraped from ½ vanilla pod

Pour 300ml of water into a small saucepan and bring to the boil over a high heat. Add the figs, reduce the heat to low and simmer gently for 10 minutes until the figs have softened further. Remove from the pan and set aside, reserving the cooking water.

Measure out 200ml of the cooking water and discard any excess (or top up with fresh water if you need to). Pour the water back into the pan. To make the confit syrup, add the panela and yacon syrup (or alternatives) into the pan and place over a medium heat. Add the star anise, cinnamon, orange zest and fig leaves and bring to the boil. Reduce the heat to low and simmer for 5 minutes, until starting to thicken, then remove from the heat and set aside to allow the flavours to infuse as the syrup cools.

When the mixture is cool, add the softened figs. Put the pan over a high heat and bring it back to the boil. Reduce the heat to low and simmer the figs in the syrup for 20 minutes until the figs are very soft and glossy and the syrup is well reduced. Discard the fig leaves, cinnamon stick, orange zest and star anise, then remove the figs to a side plate using a slotted spoon. (You can keep the syrup in an airtight jar in the fridge for up to 2 weeks.)

Put all the mascarpone vanilla cream ingredients in a bowl and whisk until the mixture has thickened and forms soft peaks.

To serve, put 2 figs in a bowl, spoon over a quarter of the syrup, top with a quarter of the mascarpone and decorate with a few extra slices of fresh fig. Repeat with the remaining ingredients.

Note: If you prefer, you can serve the figs in syrup with mozzarella, burrata or fresco cheese, instead of the vanilla cream.

Dulce con Café y Maracuyá

SERVES 6

Chocolate & Coffee Dirt with Passion Fruit. *This dessert always delights – from above it looks like a field with a sprinkling of flowers and, once you dip in your spoon, you'll find an utterly delicious and indulgent combination of fruit, chocolate and coffee. Originally, this recipe used tumbo, which is a fruit native to Peru. However, passion fruit will do very nicely.*

200ml double cream

300g dulce de leche

3 egg whites

A few edible flowers and basil micro herbs, to serve

Salt

For the passion fruit sauce

100g passion fruit purée

40g yacon syrup or caster sugar

For the edible dirt

75g cornflour

50g quinoa flour

½ tsp baking powder

35g caster sugar

50g butter, cubed and chilled

1 egg yolk

½ tsp vanilla extract

1 tbsp hazelnut milk

2 tsp cocoa powder

2 tsp instant espresso powder

Put the cream in a bowl and whisk until it forms soft peaks. Add the dulce de leche and a pinch of salt and stir gently until well combined, trying not to knock out too much air.

In a separate bowl, whisk the egg whites until they form stiff peaks. Fold a large spoonful of the egg white into the cream mixture to loosen, then fold in the rest, again making sure you keep in as much air as possible. Cover and place the bowl in the fridge for about 20 minutes until well chilled.

Meanwhile, make the passion fruit sauce. Put the passion fruit purée and the syrup or sugar in a small saucepan over a low heat. Heat gently, stirring until the sugar (if using) has dissolved, then increase the heat to medium and reduce the liquid until the sauce is the consistency of a thick syrup (about 4–5 minutes).

To make the edible dirt, preheat the oven to 150°C (gas mark 2). Mix together the cornflour, quinoa flour, baking powder and caster sugar in a bowl with a pinch of salt. Rub in the butter until the mixture resembles fine breadcrumbs. Add the egg yolk, vanilla extract and milk and combine to form a smooth dough.

Roll the dough between 2 sheets of greaseproof paper as thinly as possible, then transfer to a baking tray and remove the top sheet of paper. Bake for about 20 minutes until golden brown. Remove the dirt from the oven and allow it to cool, then crumble it finely and mix with the cocoa powder and espresso powder.

To assemble the dish, spoon a portion of the mousse in the middle of a serving plate. Sprinkle over a generous quantity of the edible dirt and dab or spoon over some of the passion fruit sauce, then decorate with the edible flowers and basil micro herbs so that the dish resembles a garden.

Helado de Queso

SERVES 6–8

Cheese Ice Cream. *This dish gets its name from the way it was originally prepared by hand using a spinning metallic bucket, which formed a layer of iced cream on its edges that was then scraped off and looked like slices of cheese. It's now so popular in Arequipa that it has its very own celebration day – the fourth Sunday in January.*

1l full-fat milk

4 cloves

4 cinnamon sticks

100g desiccated coconut

1 tin of condensed milk (397g)

200g cottage cheese

A few drops of vanilla extract

Ground cinnamon, to serve

Put the milk in a saucepan with the cloves, cinnamon sticks and coconut over a medium heat. Bring to just boiling point, then reduce the heat to low and simmer very gently for 20 minutes, stirring regularly, until the flavours of the spices and coconut have infused with the milk. Remove the pan from the heat and strain the liquid through a fine sieve into a large bowl.

Stir in the condensed milk, cottage cheese and vanilla extract, then whisk until the cheese has melted into the mixture. Leave to cool, then cover and chill in the fridge for 1 hour.

If you have an ice-cream maker, transfer the chilled mixture into the drum and churn until thick, then transfer to a freezer container and leave to freeze for at least 4–5 hours. If you don't have an ice-cream maker, put the mixture in a shallow freezer container and put in the freezer for 30 minutes. Remove the container from the freezer and beat with a hand-held electric whisk to break up the ice crystals, then return to the freezer. Repeat every 30 minutes until the ice cream is smooth and frozen.

Transfer the ice cream to the fridge 30 minutes before serving to soften up a little. Serve in scoops, sprinkled with a little ground cinnamon.

Flan de Quinua con Frutas Secas

SERVES 4

Quinoa Pannacotta with Infused Dried Fruits. *Walk through any market in any major city in the Andes and you will come across stalls selling desserts in every hue. Seek out the least colourful, as these are always more natural-tasting – and you may even be lucky enough to find a version of our quinoa pannacotta. This recipe is a delicate and sophisticated take on a classic, with deep texture and flavour.*

50g white quinoa

300ml full-fat milk

300ml whipping cream

4 egg yolks

20g cornflour

10g white quinoa flour

150g caster sugar

2 gelatine sheets

120ml physalis coulis (see p.26), to serve

For the infused dried fruits

150g caster sugar

100g dried figs

50g sultanas

100g unsulphured dried apricots

200ml pisco or vodka

First, make the infused dried fruits. Put the caster sugar in a small saucepan and pour over 150ml of water. Put the pan over a low heat and heat gently, stirring continuously, until the sugar dissolves completely. Add the fruits, stir to combine, then remove from the heat and allow to cool completely. When cold, add the pisco or vodka and stir to combine. Set aside.

Rinse the white quinoa in plenty of running water. Drain as much as possible, then transfer to a frying pan. Dry fry for 3–4 minutes until the quinoa is toasted and giving off a nutty aroma. Remove from the pan and allow to cool.

Put the milk and cream in a saucepan over a medium heat. Bring almost to the boil (about 2–3 minutes), then remove from the heat. Add the toasted quinoa to the milk and cream mixture, stir to combine and leave in the pan to infuse for about 2 hours.

Meanwhile, mix the egg yolks, cornflour, quinoa flour and caster sugar in a bowl. Whisk until the sugar has completely dissolved and the mixture is pale.

When infused, return the cream and quinoa mixture to a medium heat and bring almost to the boil. Pour half the mixture into the bowl with the egg mixture, whisking continuously, then pour everything back into the saucepan. Bring the liquid back to the boil, stirring continuously. Remove from the heat and set aside.

Soak the gelatine sheets in cold water. When they have softened, wring them out and add them to the cream and quinoa mixture. Allow the gelatine to dissolve, then push everything through a very fine sieve into a measuring jug. Pour the liquid into 1 large, 4 individual or 16 small pannacotta moulds.

Place the mould(s) in the fridge to set for at least 4 hours, or ideally overnight. Serve in equal portions drizzled with the physalis coulis and the infused dried fruits scattered over.

Vegetarian, Gluten-free

Camotillo

SERVES 8

Sweet Potato Candy. *From oca to mashua, tocosh to olluco, and chuño to any other of the many Peruvian potatoes, tubers in the Andes can make great desserts. Sweet potato is especially delicious and versatile. This camotillo is a traditional recipe that is served during festivals, at home and from street stalls across the country. Aim for the texture of soft marzipan.*

500g sweet potatoes (about 4 small sweet potatoes)

About 150g caster sugar or 80g yacon syrup

Zest of 1 orange

¼ tsp ground cinnamon

1 tbsp hundreds and thousands

Coconut or vanilla ice cream, to serve (optional)

Preheat the oven to 180°C (gas mark 4).

Roast the sweet potatoes in their skins, for about 45 minutes if small, longer if they are larger, until the flesh is soft (the long cooking time will help to dry them out well). Remove the potatoes from the oven and when they are cool enough to handle, peel and mash the flesh to a smooth purée.

Reduce the oven temperature to 150°C (gas mark 2).

Weigh the sweet potato flesh and put it in a saucepan. Add half the weight of the sweet potatoes in sugar or a quarter of the weight in yacon syrup, along with the orange zest and cinnamon. Cook over a low heat for about 5 minutes until the sugar (if using) has dissolved, then cook for 20 minutes, stirring continuously, until the mixture has reduced to the consistency of puréed potato. Remove from the heat and allow to cool.

Spoon the cooled sweet potato mixture into a piping bag. Pipe lozenges the size of dates onto a nonstick baking tray, continuing until you have used up all the mixture. Alternatively, use a dessert spoon to make quenelles.

Place on a baking tray and bake until the mixture has set round the edges but is still soft and squidgy in the middle (about 25–30 minutes). Remove the sweet potato candies from the oven and while they are still warm, sprinkle with the hundreds and thousands. You can eat them warm or cold on their own, or serve them warm with coconut or vanilla ice cream.

Gelatina de Pata

SERVES 4–6

Cow's Foot Jelly. *Most supermarket jelly is made from animal extract, so think of this as a natural version with no additives or preservatives. This recipe has remained unchanged for thousands of years and I think the most delicious examples are to be found in Huancayo's main food market. Ask your butcher to cut the cow's foot in half to make it more manageable for cooking.*

1 cow's foot, thoroughly washed and preferably cut in half

250g light soft brown sugar or 150g yacon syrup

2 cinnamon sticks

3 cloves

4 ripe figs

4 fig leaves (optional)

Pared zest of ½ orange

For the orange slices & syrup

2 oranges

200g caster sugar

150ml freshly squeezed orange juice

Place the cow's foot in a saucepan and cover with water. Bring to a rolling boil over a high heat, then start skimming off any mushroom-coloured foam that collects on the surface. Keep skimming away until the foam becomes white. Drain the cow's foot and give the pieces another wash, then put them back in the pan and cover with water again. Bring the water to the boil again, then reduce the heat to very low and simmer for about 4 hours until the cow's foot is very tender and has given out its gelatine.

Strain the liquid through a fine sieve, then line the sieve with muslin or kitchen paper and strain again into a measuring jug. Allow to cool, then skim off any fat that collects at the top.

Measure 600ml of the liquid into a saucepan. Put over a high heat and add all the remaining ingredients. Bring to the boil, then cover, reduce the heat to low and simmer gently for about 30 minutes until the flavours have infused the cow's foot liquid. Strain the liquid through a fine sieve, and again, through a sieve lined with muslin or kitchen paper into a measuring jug. Pour the liquid into 1 large jelly mould or 4–6 individual moulds or glasses. Leave for 2 hours to chill.

To make the orange slices, zest one of the oranges and reserve the zest. Top and tail both oranges so that they will sit flat on your chopping board, then cut away the peel, carefully retaining the roundness of the orange. Turn the oranges onto their sides and slice the flesh into rounds, flicking out any seeds as you go. Put the orange rounds in a bowl and set aside.

Make a syrup: put the reserved orange zest in a pan with the sugar, orange juice and 100ml of water over a low heat. Stir for 2–3 minutes until the sugar has dissolved, then turn up the heat boil for 2–3 minutes until the liquid has reduced to a syrup. Remove from the heat and cool completely. Serve the jelly with the orange slices on the side and the syrup poured over.

Humitas

SERVES 4

Purple Sweet Steamed Dumplings. *Humitas, a great street food, are steamed sweet tamales made from corn. Here, we have added a blackberry compote, but you could add any syrup, honey or sweet topping. Serving with some crème fraîche or vanilla ice cream adds that final layer of indulgence.*

175g sweetcorn kernels

50ml almond milk

2 tbsp honey, or 1 tbsp blackberry compote syrup (see below) if you don't have purple corn flour

25g cornmeal

50g purple corn flour or cornmeal

25g yacon syrup or caster sugar

1 tbsp vegetable oil or melted butter

1½ tsp chia seeds

8 corn husks, soaked in warm water for 1 hour, then drained

Spoonfuls of crème fraîche or scoops of vanilla ice cream, to serve

For the blackberry compote

200g blackberries

1 quantity of chancaca syrup (see p.120)

First, make the blackberry compote. Put the blackberries in a saucepan and pour over the syrup. Put over a low heat and warm through for 4–5 minutes until the blackberries have bled their colour into the syrup. Set aside.

Put the sweetcorn, almond milk and honey or blackberry compote syrup in a food processor or blender and blitz to smooth purée. Transfer to a bowl and stir in all the remaining ingredients except the corn husks and the crème fraîche or ice cream.

Overlap 2 corn husks widthways and put a quarter of the corn batter in the middle. Smooth out, then wrap into a neat, airtight parcel (you don't want any water to get in). Repeat with the remaining husks and batter.

Place the parcels in a steamer and steam for 1 hour to cook through. Serve hot, in the husks for your guests to unwrap, with the blackberry compote and either crème fraîche or vanilla ice cream on the side.

Helado de Sauco

SERVES 6–8

Elderberry Ice Cream. *The elder is native to the Americas and its flowers and fruit grow in plentiful supply in the Peruvian Andes. They are traditionally used for desserts and brews, and in baked pastries and cakes. In particular, I like to use them to make ice cream.*

500ml elderberry juice

50ml elderflower cordial

200ml full-fat milk

250ml double cream

2 tbsp honey

3 egg yolks

50g caster sugar

Put the elderberry juice in a saucepan over a high heat and bring to the boil. Reduce the heat to low and simmer for about 10 minutes until the liquid has reduced by half. Remove from the heat, allow to cool and then stir in the cordial. Set aside.

In a separate saucepan, combine the milk, cream and honey. Put over a low heat and warm slowly, stirring, until the honey has melted (about 2–3 minutes). Increase the heat, and bring the liquid almost to the boil, then remove from the heat.

Whisk the egg yolks and sugar together in a large bowl until very pale and mousse-like. Pour the milk mixture over the egg and sugar mixture in a long, slow stream, stirring continuously, until it's all combined. Then, pour everything back into the saucepan and put the pan over a low–medium heat for 10–12 minutes, stirring continuously, until the mixture has thickened enough to coat the back of a spoon and you can draw a line through it.

Remove the pan from the heat and pass the custard through a sieve into a bowl. Add the elderberry and elderflower reduction to the bowl, then use a hand-held electric whisk to whisk it up for 2–3 minutes until well aerated. Allow the mixture to cool, then transfer to an ice-cream maker, if you have one. Churn until the mixture has thickened, then transfer to a freezer container and freeze for at least 4–5 hours. If you don't have an ice-cream maker, put the mixture in a shallow freezer container and put in the freezer for 30 minutes. Remove the container from the freezer and beat with a hand-held electric whisk to break up the ice crystals, then return to the freezer. Repeat every 30 minutes until the ice cream is smooth and frozen.

Transfer the ice cream to the fridge 30 minutes before serving to soften up a little.

Vegetarian, Gluten-free

Brownie de Choco-Quinua

SERVES 12–16

Chocolate Quinoa Brownie. *This is a protein-rich brownie that has tons of crunch and plenty of bite. It's one of the most popular desserts available at Andina, and one that has inspired chefs at many other restaurants, too. You can use a little more black quinoa for added texture, if you like.*

100g uncooked mixed quinoa (red, black and white)

175g plain flour

50g quinoa flour

200g butter, chilled and cut into small cubes

150ml full-fat milk

300g dark chocolate (at least 70% cocoa solids), broken into squares

4 eggs

250g yacon syrup or light soft brown sugar

Salt

First, cook the quinoa. Rinse it thoroughly under cold water and put it in a saucepan. Cover with fresh water, put over a high heat and bring to the boil. Reduce the heat to low, then cover and simmer for 20 minutes, or until the quinoa tail has unfurled and the grains are very tender. Be careful to check the red and black quinoa are done as they can take a little longer than the white. Drain the quinoa, then lay it out on a tray and allow to cool and dry out a little.

Preheat the oven to 160°C (gas mark 2–3). Grease and line a 20x30cm brownie tin, or spray it with cake-release spray. Mix the plain flour, quinoa flour and a pinch of salt together in a bowl and set aside.

Put the butter and milk in a saucepan over a low heat and heat gently until the butter has melted. Remove the pan from the heat and add all the chocolate. Whisk until the chocolate has melted and the mixture has emulsified and formed a ganache.

In a separate bowl, use a hand-held electric whisk to whisk together the eggs and syrup or sugar (you can use a stand mixer if you prefer) until the sugar (if using) has dissolved and the mixture is pale and mousse-like. Pour the ganache around the edges of the sweet egg mixture, then add the flour mixture. Fold everything together very gently, being careful not to overwork the batter, then add the cooked quinoa and mix again.

Scrape the mixture into the prepared brownie tin and bake in the oven for 20–25 minutes, making sure you check for doneness after 20 minutes – the cake should still be slightly squidgy in the middle (it will firm up a little as it cools). Remove the brownie from the oven and allow it to cool in the tin, then cut it into 12–16 pieces for everyone to help themselves.

Shtrukala de Oxapampa

SERVES 6–8

Oxapampa Tart. *Thanks to migration from Austria and Germany to the Pasco region in the Andes many decades ago, Peruvians are lucky enough to have this sticky and dramatic dessert. Here, we've made it using plantain, but you can use any kind of banana. Serve it with single cream or ice cream.*

For the pastry

35g white quinoa flour

50g gram flour

150g gluten-free flour

125g butter, softened

50g icing sugar

25g muscovado sugar

3 egg yolks

For the filling

15g butter

2 small or 1 large, ripe plantain, peeled and diced

1 medium–large banana, peeled and mashed

75g mascarpone

2 eggs

For the plantain slices

1 small green plantain, peeled and cut in half

1 cinnamon stick

3 star anise

½ tsp bicarbonate of soda

For the butterscotch

150g caster sugar

50g butter

100ml chancaca syrup (see p.120)

First, make the pastry. Mix all the flours together in a bowl. In a separate bowl, beat together the butter and sugars until soft and mousse-like. Add 1 egg yolk to the creamed butter and sugar, then a spoonful of flour mixture and stir to incorporate. Repeat for the remaining egg yolks, alternating with a spoonful of flour each time. Add the remaining flour, stir to combine and form into a soft ball. Wrap in clingfilm and chill until needed.

To make the filling, melt the butter in a small frying pan over a low heat. Add the plantain and fry, stirring, for 4–5 minutes until the plantain dice are lightly golden brown. Remove from the heat and allow to cool. Transfer to a food processor or blender, add the banana and blitz to a purée. Add the mascarpone and eggs and blitz again to a smooth, pourable mixture. Set aside.

To make the plantain slices, put the plantain halves in a saucepan and cover with water. Put over a high heat. Add the cinnamon and star anise and bring to the boil. Add the bicarbonate of soda, then reduce the heat and simmer for about 15 minutes until al dente. Drain and slice the plantain into 1cm-thick rings. Set aside.

To make the butterscotch, melt the sugar in a heavy-based saucepan over a medium heat, shaking it so that it covers the base evenly and resisting the urge to stir. When the melted sugar has turned a light golden brown (about 6–7 minutes), reduce the heat, then add the butter. Whisk to a smooth sauce, then add the chancaca syrup. Whisk again to a rich caramel. Set aside.

Preheat the oven to 170°C (gas mark 3). Take a 23cm diameter nonstick ovenproof skillet or shallow nonstick tin. Pour in the butterscotch, then top with the plantain slices and cover with the filling. Roll out the pastry, placing it on top of the filling to cover and tucking the edges down. Cut a couple of slits in the dough.

Bake in the oven for 30 minutes, or until the pastry is golden brown. Leave to rest for 1 minute, then turn out the tart onto a plate and serve in slices.

Vegetarian, Gluten-free

Bebidas

DRINKS

Homenaje al Mate de Coca

SERVES 4

2g linden or lime-leaf tea

2g boldo leaves or 1g dried bay leaves, crumbled

2g Sencha tea (whole-leaf green tea)

½ tbsp maca powder

Honey (optional), to serve

Homage to Coca Tea. *If you have coca leaves, place about 6 leaves per person in a cup with boiling water and brew for 3 minutes, then serve. If not, here's an alternative version.*

Put 1 litre of water in a saucepan and bring to the boil over a high heat. Add all the leaves and the maca powder to the water, reduce the heat to low and simmer for 5 minutes. Strain and serve hot, with honey to sweeten, if desired.

Vegetarian, Gluten-free

Ponche de Arguedas

SERVES 2

50g white sesame seeds

50g whole almonds

50g raw peanuts

50g walnuts

50g desiccated coconut

1 cinnamon stick

1 clove

100ml almond milk

A few drops of vanilla extract

2 tbsp yacon or maple syrup

40ml pisco or vodka

Arguedas' Hot Nut Punch. *Ponches are made with many different types of nut, bean, corn, fruit and vegetable, but this ponche from Apurímac is my favourite. As Apurímac is the birthplace of José María Arguedas, my favourite Peruvian writer, I named this recipe after him.*

Put the sesame seeds, almonds, peanuts, walnuts and coconut into a food processor or blender with 500ml of water. Blitz for 10 seconds, then transfer to a saucepan and add the cinnamon stick and clove. Bring to the boil over a high heat, then reduce the heat to low and simmer for 10 minutes.

Strain the liquid through a fine sieve into a bowl or jug, then transfer the strained liquid back into the saucepan and add the almond milk, vanilla and syrup. Reheat until piping hot, then stir in the pisco or vodka and serve immediately.

Vegetarian, Vegan, Gluten-free

Chicha Enamorada

SERVES 2

1 purple corn cob, or corn-on-the-cob and 200g blackberries

4 small pieces of pineapple skin

½ apple, unpeeled and diced

½ quince, unpeeled and diced

100ml freshly squeezed orange juice

1 clove

1 cinnamon stick

90–120ml yacon or maple syrup, plus extra to taste, if necessary

Juice of 1 lime, plus slices of lime, to serve

Purple Refresher. *Purple corn, traditionally used for this drink, is difficult to find, so here's a version that you can enjoy during late summer and autumn when you can create the colour using fresh blackberries (or at other times of year using frozen).*

Put 750ml of water in a large saucepan over a high heat. Add the purple maize or the corn and blackberries, along with the pineapple skin, apple, quince, orange juice, and spices. Bring to the boil, then reduce the heat to very low and simmer for 30 minutes until the liquid has turned a deep purple and taken on the flavour of the fruit and spices.

Remove the pan from the heat and stir in the syrup. Taste and add a little more if you prefer it sweeter. Leave the flavours to infuse while the mixture cools. When cool, strain the liquid, add the lime juice and serve over ice with slices of lime.

Vegetarian, Vegan, Gluten-free

Emoliente de Casita Andina

SERVES 2

10g barley

10g linseeds

2g chamomile tea

2g dried horsetail

¼ small pineapple, peeled and roughly chopped

Peel from ¼ apple

1 tbsp quince jelly or membrillo

A squeeze of lime, to serve

Yacon or maple syrup (optional)

Casita Andina Tea. *As the sun rises on every street corner of the central Andina towns, so do emolienteras. These are ladies selling hot teas in many flavours, and with special ingredients that give a healthy boost. This recipe is a Casita Andina favourite. We like it cold and refreshing, but you can serve and drink it warm, if you prefer.*

Put the barley in a dry frying pan and toast over a medium heat for 45 minutes until it is nutty and aromatic.

Put 750ml of water in a saucepan over a high heat. Add all the ingredients, including the toasted barley (but except the lime and yacon or maple syrup), and stir until the quince jelly or membrillo has dissolved. Bring to the boil, then reduce the heat to low and simmer for 20 minutes.

Strain the liquid and divide it between 2 mugs. To serve, add a squeeze of lime, and a little syrup to sweeten, if you like.

Vegetarian, Vegan

Chicha

SERVES 2

Corn Brew. *Meet Mónica Huerta Alpaca, Arequipa's master Chicha de Guiñapo brewer, lovingly making her own version of this iconic Andina drink. Guiñapo is a purple corn, but you can use any type of corn you can get hold of. Every corn is different, so think trial and error – the results will be worth it. If you want to give your brew a twist reminiscent of those in Cusco, before drinking add a handful of strawberries and blend.*

250g jora or guiñapo corn kernels or sweetcorn kernels

125g barley

50g panela, palm sugar, jaggery or light soft brown sugar

1 tsp cloves

Granulated sugar (optional), to taste

Soak the corn or sweetcorn in water, then roughly drain (the kernels should be wet) and spread them over a baking tray. Cover the kernels with wet kitchen paper or a wet tea towel, then leave them somewhere warm for 3 days to germinate – an airing cupboard is ideal. Make sure the paper or towel stays damp – splash with water if necessary. The kernels are ready when they have started to sprout shoots.

Transfer the sprouted kernels to a clean baking tray. Preheat the oven to its lowest temperature, then put the kernels in the oven until they have dried out completely (at least 4 hours). Remove from the oven and allow to cool down.

Put the barley in a large frying pan and toast over a medium heat for 4–5 minutes until well toasted and aromatic. Set aside.

Put 2 litres of water in a large saucepan over a high heat and bring to the boil. Add the dried kernels and the toasted barley and return to the boil, then reduce the heat to low and simmer for 20 minutes. Add a further 1 litre of water, along with the 50g of sugar and the cloves, then simmer, covered, very gently for 2 hours to allow the flavours to mingle. Remove the pan from the heat and allow to cool until lukewarm.

Strain the liquid through a muslin cloth into either a fermentation container (one with a fermentation seal that will let carbon dioxide escape from the container) or a container that you can cover with a layer of muslin. If using the latter, tie the muslin firmly in place. Leave in a cool, dark place for at least 5 days, to allow the mixture to ferment (in a fermentation container, bubbles will stop rising through the airlock when the brew is ready). Strain through a muslin cloth again and decant into sterilized bottles. Serve sweetened with sugar, if you prefer.

Licuado Vallejo

SERVES 2

½ ripe avocado, flesh roughly chopped

300ml pear juice

50ml lime juice

20 mint leaves, plus 2 sprigs to decorate

A large handful of baby spinach leaves

Vallejo's Smoothie. *Named in memory of the awesome Andina poet César Vallejo, this perfect green smoothie has been on our menu since we opened Andina. We change our menu frequently, but this recipe is uncomplicated, unadulterated and light (and it has an eye-popping bright green colour), and that makes it enduring.*

Put all the ingredients into a food processor or blender with 100ml of water and a few ice cubes. Blitz until very smooth. Serve in 2 tall glasses or large tumblers and decorate each serving with a sprig of mint. Serve immediately.

Vegetarian, Vegan, Gluten-free

Licuado Pimientolada

SERVES 2

1 banana

½ red pepper, deseeded and roughly chopped

200ml fresh pineapple juice

100ml pressed apple juice

50ml coconut cream

Red Pepper, Coconut & Banana Smoothie. *When I first tried this, I can honestly say I had never had anything like it before. With red pepper playing a leading role, the combination of ingredients is simple yet remarkable.*

Put all the ingredients in a food processor or blender with 8 ice cubes and blitz until smooth. Pour into 2 tall glasses or large tumblers and serve immediately.

Vegetarian, Vegan, Gluten-free

Licuado Zarzamaca

SERVES 2

20 blueberries, plus 2 extra to decorate

6 blackberries

1 banana

1 tsp maca powder

100ml pressed apple juice

Blueberry & Maca Smoothie. *This revitalizing drink came about when our Head of Bars, Miguel Arbe, won a bet to create an all-day refreshing and filling smoothie.*

Put all the ingredients in a food processor or blender with 10 ice cubes and blitz until smooth. Serve in 2 tall glasses or large tumblers and decorate each serving with a whole blueberry.

Vegetarian, Vegan, Gluten-free

Batido Chaska

SERVES 2

3 dried ready-to-eat figs

½ banana

30g lucuma purée; or 10g lucuma powder, mixed with 20ml of any type of milk

300ml pressed apple juice

200ml quinoa, almond or semi-skimmed milk

Yacon or maple syrup, to serve (optional)

Slices of dried fig, to decorate

Fig, Banana & Lucuma Shake. *The name of this shake is the Quechua for the word 'star'. The drink is energizing for any time of day, but especially in the early morning. Our Andina drinks' maestro, Jarek Kaszynski, who opens Andina for breakfast, has become a bit of a legend in East London – partly because of his enduring positivity, but also because he is the man who rustles up this wake-up call.*

Put all the ingredients except the syrup and slices of dried fig into a food processor or blender and blitz until as smooth as it can be – the fig seeds will resist! Pour over ice into 2 tall glasses or large tumblers and drizzle over a little syrup if you wish. Decorate each glass with a slice of dried fig and serve immediately.

Vegetarian, Gluten-free

Batido Perú Poderoso

SERVES 2

1 banana

4 ready-to-eat dried figs

1 tsp cocoa nibs or cocoa powder

300ml soya milk

1 tsp chia seeds

A few coffee beans, to decorate

Peru Power Shake. *A simple and super-quick pick-me-up, this drink is loved by our customers, especially post-exercise. Make sure the chia seeds are fully blitzed so that the blend is completely smooth.*

Put all the ingredients in a food processor or blender with 10 cubes of ice and blitz until smooth. Serve in 2 tall glasses or large tumblers decorated with the coffee beans.

Vegetarian, Vegan, Gluten-free

Altiplano

SERVES 2

Highland Aperitif. *Casita Andina's much-loved cocktail is a refreshing tipple for any time of the day. The herb and lime marmalade on the rim ensures a sweet entrance before a zesty passion-fruit kick and the hit of aromatic Torontel grape pisco.*

100ml Torontel grape pisco

60ml passion fruit juice

25ml sugar syrup or 3 tbsp yacon syrup

200ml tonic water

Aronia or blueberry juice (optional)

For the huacatay-lime marmalade

8–10 huacatay leaves, or a couple of leaves each of mint, parsley, coriander and tarragon, finely chopped

4 tbsp lime marmalade

First, make the huacatay-lime marmalade. Blitz the herbs with the lime marmalade in a mini-processor (or in a small bowl using a stick blender) until as smooth as possible. Set aside.

Fill a cocktail shaker with ice. Add the pisco, passion fruit juice and syrup. Shake for at least 30 seconds.

Rim 2 old-fashioned glasses with the huacatay-lime marmalade.

Strain half the mixture into each glass, then top up the glasses with the tonic water. Add a dash of aronia or blueberry juice, if using, and serve immediately.

Vegetarian, Vegan, Gluten-free

TRIBUIDORA
PE GAS
9676
FISE
Lima Gas
REPSOL
DESAYUNO
* Lomo saltado
* pollo al Horno
* pollo Dorado c/n papas
* Chuleta c/n papas
* Arroz a la Cubana
* Tortilla de verduras
avena, te, cafe
aniz manzanilla
Jugos

Ecuador

Colombia

Brazil

Océano
Pacífico

1 CAJAMARCA
2 LA LIBERTAD
3

HUÁNUCO
4

PASCO 6
5

7
8
9

LIMA JUNÍN

11
10

HUANCAVELICA

12
13
14

CUSCO

15
16 APURÍMAC
17

AYACUCHO

PUNO

AREQUIPA
18 19 20

Bolivia

Chile

1 CAJAMARCA
2 OTUZCO
3 SANTIAGO DE CHUCO
4 HUÁNUCO
5 OXAPAMPA
6 CERRO DE PASCO
7 JAUJA
8 INGENIO
9 HUANCAYO
10 HUANCAVELICA
11 SANTO TOMÁS DE PATA
12 MACHU PICCHU
13 OLLANTAYTAMBO
14 CUSCO
15 ABANCAY
16 AYACUCHO
17 VITO
18 AREQUIPA
19 PUNO
20 LAKE TITICACA

N
W   E
S

THE COAST   THE ANDES   THE AMAZON

Relatos

STORIES FROM
THE ANDINA REGIONS

HUANCAVELICA

Feli's strong arms gripped me in the most moving bear hug, squeezing out my tears of loss – circumstance was robbing me of her and almost everything I knew. By 1984, when I was 11 years old, the Shining Path had threatened my father and he was ready to leave Peru to seek a safer home for my sister and me. Feli, whom I called 'auntie' but who was our housekeeper, was one of the people I was going to miss most. Such was my attachment to her that my mother, also staying behind in Peru, had to wrench me from her arms. My connection to the region of Huancavelica is deeply personal, because it connects me to Feli.

Feli is short for Felicitas. In ancient Roman culture, *felicitas* (from the Latin *felix*, meaning 'fruitful, blessed, happy, lucky') is a condition of divinely inspired productivity, blessedness or happiness. Hers was always to be a positive significance in my life. I was five when I first met her. She worked as a housekeeper with our neighbours next door; they had a beautiful garden. One sunny day I saw Feli in the garden and asked her to give me some flowers to take to school to give to my friends. That's how she recalls first meeting me. A year later she was taking care of me and working with our family.

Wise, caring and loving, she had wide, smiling eyes, kisses that made my cheeks pop, and hair thick as wire tied in a bun like a Japanese Geisha. She seemed very tall to my little self, and broad, with calves that any athlete would be proud of. She was a true Andina: powerful and built for hard times; ancient times. She was born in the 40s in the village of Santo Tomás de Pata, high up in the mountains of Huancavelica. This was a barren land, so cold that crops found it hard to bear fruit, and so high that the sun blistered its inhabitants' dark skins. Born into a family of three brothers and sisters, her parents were farmers and she grew up living among the cows, horses, donkeys and sheep, and the crops of corn, potatoes and quinoa. The nearest school was two hours' walk away and Feli spent much of her childhood walking and working, developing those strong calves. Her home

was typical of those in her village, with no running water or electricity – which remains true even today in this poor, forgotten mountaintop corner of Peru.

Like many in her village, she dreamed of leaving and going to Lima – the Peruvian capital and supposed land of plenty. So, aged 18 and on her own, Feli left behind the harsh reality of everything she knew and headed for the humidity of Lima. There, she found work cleaning and housekeeping. She created a home in a mud hut on a plot of land near our house, where she lived among turkeys, dogs and allotments, and where for the first ten years, still she had no electricity or water. She worked in many places until she found me. I say found, because I was lost and slightly forgotten, too. My mum and dad were seldom at home, and when they were there, they would argue and sometimes fight. Feli became my world; she was pure light, and her cooking carried that special ingredient *cariño*, or care and love. I ate everything she fed me, every last morsel. For all her faults my mother did care about eating well, so she asked Feli to feed me healthy food: pulses, quinoa, beans. Anything but chips. And Feli's seasoning was spot on.

Sadly, as a result of my mum's strict diet, we never got to try the many local dishes Feli would talk about. The hearty Patasca (p.158), a slow-cooked stewy soup with its tripe, mote corn and cow's foot mix to me sounded exotic. The flavourful El Puchero (see p.167), another *campesino* (peasant) soup, made for those long winter days from January to March when the vegetables are in season. But above all she spoke of the Pachamanca (p.109). Feli tempted me with these delights and through the years I've sought out her different dishes, not only to try them, but also to learn how to make them; it is with extreme excitement that I present them here, in homage to Feli, in my book.

Eggs were the first thing I learnt how to cook, the first ingredient I really mastered: poached, fried, boiled. Feli taught me. One day, I realized I was eating so many eggs and my repertoire was getting limited. So much so that I cheekily said to her, '*Oye Feli, si solo hago huevos día y noche, me voy a convertir en huevón!*' Which means something like 'Hey Feli, if I can only cook eggs day and night, I'm going to turn into an idiot!' The word *huevón* had a double meaning, much stronger than just 'egghead'. She would laugh, and I felt completely protected by her. She was dark skinned, and always smiling, considered, measured, careful, caring, loving, warm, indigenous. She embodied the Andina spirit. Another mother of mine, this time from Huancavelica.

She'd talk a lot about her home. Located in the heart of the Peruvian Andes, with almost half a million people, Huancavelica is one of the oldest and coldest regions in Peru. It is surrounded by majestic high mountains with snow-capped peaks, and is peppered with deserted lush plains, beautiful blue-and-green lagoons and hot thermal springs. This was the home of the farmers and warriors known as the Wari, then the Chanca and then the Huanca people. Some say Huancavelica's name comes from combining the Quechua words *huanca* and *huilka*, which together mean 'Idol of Stone'. But I prefer the story that tells of a dazzling Huanca lady called Isabel, whom the locals lovingly referred to as 'Isabelica' (little Isabel), or simply 'Belica' – giving us, of course, *Huanca Belica*. The vast majority of Huancavelica's people are indigenous – far greater numbers speak traditional Quechua than Spanish. Peru's number-one potato producer, the region also grows great quantities of peas and barley, and a variety of beans; there is farming of trout, beef, pork, lamb and alpaca.

Its capital city, also called Huancavelica, with its beautiful colonial main square, was founded in 1571 when the Spanish discovered mercury there, itself crucial for the extraction of silver. But mining was a treacherous endeavour and the exploitation of miners was rife. Cruel mining practices have cost the lives of many thousands of Andinos over the centuries. Notwithstanding, through the sweat, the blood and the bodies of Huancavelica's people, the region became home to the colonialist Santa Barbara mine, famous throughout the world and acknowledged as a pillar that supported the Spanish Empire.

But this was all before Feli's time. The early 20th century brought both intense drought and devastating floods to Huancavelica, ripping through the heart of the agricultural community. Mining continued at the hands of foreigners, and local Andinos were left forgotten. Then, in the latter 20th century, the fierce Shining Path arrived from neighbouring Ayacucho (p.227), causing further mayhem and horror. For several years terrorists or the military took over many towns and cities. With their humble region now the scene of war, during the 80s many in Huancavelica began a mass migration to Lima.

It is then, against this backdrop, that Feli became a part of our family. I remember clearly the day when we discovered that more than 200 people had been rounded up and murdered in her village; a village that the day before had only 250 inhabitants. Her mother and sister escaped; her many cousins and uncles did not. Many have yet to be found. Although Feli was safe with us during such devastating times, through her kind, smiling eyes, her face painted her pain in every look. To me, like her region's name, she was an Idol of Stone, a Wari descendant, a Quechua lady that to this day is my friend and surrogate mother.

Thankfully, since the mid-90s Huancavelica has been a place of peace. This land of farmers and miners, appreciated for its hospitable warmth, simplicity and humility, is once again blossoming, poised off the beaten track to be discovered by anyone seeking human and natural beauty. Feli carries her region's renewed positivity and confidence. When I see her on my travels back to Peru, I take her a bunch of flowers in memory of that most special of moments when we first met. Together we reminisce, and I often wonder what life would have been like if I'd stayed in Peru in 1984, with Feli by my side. Soon enough I'm sure we would have dug up the garden and cooked our own delicious *pachamanca*.

LA LIBERTAD

Located in the northwest of Peru, La Libertad (meaning 'freedom') is the only department that covers Peru's three main geographical regions: coast, mountains (80 per cent of its territory) and jungle. Its capital Trujillo is considered the city of eternal spring owing to its semi-tropical weather. Trujillo was one of the most important cities in the north of Peru during the Spanish conquest, but it was also the first to be freed, making it a key player in the later struggle for independence. The liberator General Don Simón Bolívar proclaimed, 'La Libertad has given Peru its freedom!' Hence the region's name.

La Libertad has become the third-largest regional economy in Peru through its investment in agriculture, livestock, hunting, forestry and manufacture. The largest harvested crops are sugar cane (La Libertad is the main producer in the country), rice, wheat, barley, potatoes and yellow corn. Furthermore, with high international demand for asparagus, La Libertad, with its good soil and suitable climate conditions, has become the country's leading producer of that, too. Artichokes, avocados and peppers are not far behind.

For me, though, the fact that the region's name means freedom is something of an irony. Journeys there when I was a kid, when I used to go to see my granny Mamita Naty, felt like being trapped in never-ending torture. We'd set off from Lima on a ten-hour bus ride up the Pan-American Highway. In the 80s, this single-lane, superfast road, packed with drivers who didn't look and were always in a hurry, was the site of many overturned buses and accidents that were often fatal. It frightened me and made the journey feel twice as long. Once reaching Trujillo, which was halfway through the journey, we would stay the night at some new relative's house – our family forever seemed to be extending itself. What happened next was the most arduous part: the following day we would board a bus to Santiago de Chuco, from where we would walk to Cachicadán, the hamlet where my granny lived.

Sounds straightforward, but Santiago was at least another eight hours on from Trujillo. The bus was basic, had no toilet, had sometimes a missing or broken window; the ride was always dusty and you were lucky if your seat had cushioning – most seats were merely planks of wood with a cloth on top. The bus would wind dangerously up the mountains, hugging the road and narrowly missing the precipice every few minutes. It often broke down along the way, as the dirty, pot-holed roads murdered its suspension and tyres. There was one good thing about the journey, though: the regular toilet stops, which were always in family-run roadside restaurants – the *picanterías* of La Libertad. There, I clearly remember eating delicious Shambar (p.98), or Chochoca (p.164) soup.

When I finally got to Santiago, though, I always realized how worthwhile that journey had been: this is one of the prettiest towns in La Libertad. It is also the birthplace of Peru's greatest poet César Vallejo. Born in 1892, Vallejo is considered a giant among Peru's literary figures of that time; he was also my great-great uncle and his melancholic writings, often quoted at family gatherings, haunted me as a child.

Reaching Santiago was pure joy. The air outside the bus was filled with all the aromas of delicious breads and cakes emanating from the local bakeries. Then the most wonderful bit: seeing Mamita Naty once we reached her home. On the table of her house was always a welcoming dish of *shambar*.

A true Andina, my granny was strong. She was a farmer, a bookkeeper and became Lord Mayoress of her village. She worked day and night to feed her eight children, my mother being one of them. She defied tradition and stereotype: she became a prominent politician, she refused to ride side saddle, and she was the life and soul of any party. Hers was an open house that reflected her own generosity, and her kitchen was her own *picantería*. Whenever I visited, there was always someone new sitting in there: a traveller, a local *campesino* farmer on a break, a messenger, an important local politician. Her suckling pig (p.125) and guinea-pig dishes amounted to feasts fit for a king. She bred guinea pigs in the warmth beneath her mud stove and during my visits it was my job to choose which guinea pig to butcher for our meal. She would cook it with chilli and spices, turning it into a *picante*.

My visits made us close and, when I wasn't there, she had a special way to keep in touch. When I was a young boy living in Lima, a highlight of my month was receiving an *encomienda* from my granny. This was a large basket full of ingredients – some prepared, some just as they came – from her farm: serrano ham (which from her village is spicy and hot), a creamy and strong *queso fresco* (delicious fried or eaten fresh), heavenly bread, and *rosquitas* (savoury, crunchy doughnut-shaped biscuits), *chancaca* (a sweet sugarcane sauce), *manjar blanco* (a type of milk custard) and eggs (the bluest and whitest you've ever seen, with bright orange yolks). All of these treasures we turned into dishes that not only our family, but also our friends could enjoy – in Mamita Naty's own spirit of generosity. The practice of sending *encomiendas* in Peru was a typical token of love from afar. My granny would always attach a note that read 'Con mucho cariño' – 'With lots of love' – which has now become the motto in our restaurants.

Mamita Naty passed away just a few years ago, but I still hold Santiago dear in my heart, which is why *shambar* is so special to me. It is sometimes called

Monday Soup. According to historians that's because the soup was made using the leftovers from the weekend's festivities and celebrations. The essence of the dish lies in the type of gammon or serrano ham you use: the more cured and spicy, the better.

If you go deep into La Libertad's Andes, to towns such as Santiago, Angasmarca or Otuzco, you can find great serrano hams and so also great *shambar*. A few years ago, a top British restaurant critic went to Peru. I hooked him up with my uncle, who took him to a slum where there is a La Libertad fellow who cooks a mean *shambar*. The critic came back raving about the soup, saying it was the best dish he had ever eaten. There's no doubt that that soup will have been made with the most delicious ham, but I don't think that's all the critic could taste. Stirred in, to make the soup truly great, were also history, tradition and, most of all, the secret Peruvian ingredient known as *mucho cariño* – much love – as Mamita Naty used to say.

AREQUIPA

The heart of Peruvian food is felt in all corners of the Andes: in the many markets, street stalls and restaurants, and in the aromas emanating from the kitchens inside the Andinas' homes. But, I think, the heart beats faster and louder in Arequipa than anywhere else. Here, gastronomy is the result of plentiful native ingredients, dishes and traditions; like a culinary Inca warrior, it conquers the taste buds of all who cross its path; it is living, breathing history. The sheer quantity of dishes from Arequipa is exceptional. If I found 120 recipes in books from the region of Apurímac; I found more than 600 in books from Arequipa.

The region of Arequipa stretches across the central–south Andes right up to the Pacific coast. It is a place rich in indigenous culture and tradition; a place where its early tribes were overpowered and organized by the Incas. Legend has it that in the late 13th century, the Inca Mayta Cápac was the first to settle in Arequipa, stationed there with his troops. When the time came for the troops to move on, many men asked Mayta Cápac if they could stay. 'Ari quipay,' he replied, meaning 'Yes, stay.' In time Arequipa became a melting pot of settlers from Europe, as well as *mestizos* – those of combined descent.

Like so many other cities of the Andina regions, Arequipa is the name of the region's capital city as well as of the region itself. Founded by the Spanish in 1540, the city enjoys a fine location and climate, and easy distance from both fertile lands and the coast. The city prospered, so much so that after Peru declared independence from Spain in 1821, Arequipa became the country's capital, remaining so for almost fifty years. Now, it is second only to Lima. With its stunning churches and plazas, and buildings made using volcanic white rock (earning it the nickname the 'white city'), Arequipa's old town has been declared of great importance to the Cultural Heritage of Humanity.

A key economic outpost for the colonialists, Arequipa has attracted many migrants, making it the land of opportunity within the Andes for those daring to venture from the capital city. For more than 500 years, migrants to Arequipa have brought their many influences and traditions. For me, this fusion has made it a culinary giant on the Peruvian food scene.

As in many second-largest cities (think Barcelona or Manchester), Arequipa's residents are a proud people with a fierce regional patriotism that aims to differentiate the city from Lima. I think there is a lot Arequipa can claim as unique. For a start Arequipa can boast being the origin of several of Peru's most recognizable and emblematic dishes, including the Chupe de Camarones Antiguo (p.160), which is a kind of prawn chowder, the Solterito – a delicious broad bean, queso fresco and olive salad (p.66), the Ocopa Sauce made with herbs and nuts (p.41) and the Rocoto Relleno or stuffed hot red peppers (p.107).

These were dishes my great aunts Carmela and Otilia cooked every week at home in Lima when I was a child. Today, everywhere I go I look for Carmela and Otilia. I miss them in so many ways, but most of all I miss their cooking. During all the terrorism and violence we had to live through while we were in Peru, their food provided comfort – it made me happy and gave me hope.

When I left Peru in 1984, I left Carmela and Otilia in Lima, old but alive and well. Sadly, they passed away almost a decade ago. I was not there, of course, and a part of me shall always mourn them. But, I will also always feel them with me. I see Otilia's eyes in the eyes of my own daughter, whom I named after her; I have kept Aunt Carmela alive in recipes that have been published in books and newspapers, each printing bearing her name. I have photographs of both of them all around my house. When I go back to Peru, I see them in different places: in markets, in churches, in restaurants – the places they so often took me. Above all, though, I see them through the eyes of the *picanteras*, the women chefs and mothers who hold their families together through food and love, feeding them, their friends and their customers in their *picanterías*. These traditional family-run restaurants pop up in many parts of Peru, but they appear especially in Arequipa, serving the regional versions of the dishes my great aunts used to cook. In a way these dishes are my spiritual connection to this ancestry and it is in Arequipa that I feel and hear Carmela and Otilia most.

Every time I go back to Arequipa, I'm received more and more like a prodigal son. The *picanteras* of this city have adopted me as one of their own. These exceptional women hold the secrets to traditional cooking techniques. They have set up the Picantera Society of Arequipa, a group of forty or more (mostly) women, who come together to organize and chronicle their knowledge and establish key rules on how to run a *picantería*. Their generosity and enthusiasm are both infectious and limitless.

My most recent visit to Arequipa was in the week of my birthday and I spent it at La Nueva Palomino, a *picantería* in the heart of Arequipa. It is run by the charismatic and loving Mónica Huerta Alpaca, who invited me to celebrate my birthday with her, asking several other local *picanteras* to bring a celebratory dish, too. Mónica's Chicha corn brew (p.199), which I'd go so far as to say is the best in Peru, flowed freely. We tucked into this and every other dish on offer. Every woman had chosen to cook something special – she had not only prepared it, but also offered it with love. It wasn't just what these women did to celebrate my birthday that mattered, but how they did it.

Picanterías are unique, distinguished by four things: 1. They serve *chicha*; 2. every day has its own specific *chupe* (soup); 3. they serve a variety of *picantes* (stews) and other traditional dishes; and 4. they are democratic, inclusive places where anyone from any walk of life can eat traditional food, drink *chicha* and socialize. Presidents and authors, bricklayers and lawyers, artists and dentists – all are welcome. Years ago, in fact, *picanterías* were primarily places of cultural exchange. Social gatherings, political protests, art exhibitions, poetry readings and live music all found a voice there. Now, many are attached to farms, orchards or allotments. They all use local and sustainable produce that is organically grown.

On the walls of Casita Andina hang specially commissioned portraits of four *picanteras* who have particularly inspired us: La Lucila, La Benita, La Cau Cau and La Palomino. Some of these women have now passed away, but I hope that our gesture on the walls of the restaurant keeps their spirit alive. That, and their own families back in Peru. While I was in Arequipa, I spent the day at Picantería La Lucila. Doña Lucila, who reminds me of my own great-grandmother Luchita, died just a few years ago, but Gladys and Ruth, two of Lucila's five daughters greeted me. Their kitchen is well known in Arequipa. At more than 100 years old, this kitchen has been handed down through several generations. With its whitewashed adobe walls, natural light that streams in sunbeams through a ceiling hatch, wood-burning stove and years of history etched on its walls, this kitchen embodies the real cooking of the Andes. The women have a large sink with fresh drinking water, but they have no electricity and no gas – there's not a modern-day kitchen appliance in sight. All mixing and blending is done patiently and painstakingly by hand using the traditional *batán*. This is a giant moon-shaped smooth stone that the cook rocks from side to side over a flat boulder, using it as a grinder, a mill and a pestle and mortar. Lucila's daughters use the same *batán* that has been used since the opening of their *picantería*, and it holds the key to their slow, fresh cooking that places no importance on time. Cooking is unrushed; tradition and flavour come first.

Preparation starts at dawn, with the first dishes arriving on the table at 11am. The women keep going until the food runs out, or the *picantería* closes at late afternoon. When I was there I sat at the kitchen table and watched how Gladys spent an hour using the *batán* to make a traditional Ocopa Sauce (p.41), while Ruth fed me carrot fritters (p.47), and let me try some exquisite salads – Sarza de Patitas (p.61) and Sarza de Criadillas (p.68), all washed down with *chicha*. I was intrigued by their raw prawn dishes, such as Sivinche (p.76), a kind of spicy prawn tartare, and Celador de Camarones (p.85), which is like a raw prawn ceviche. Packed with flavour and character, these are ancestral dishes that are hard to find outside Arequipa – which is all the more reason to have included them in this book.

While I sat there watching these women and tasting their beautiful food, I became aware of the utter importance of this restaurant and all the restaurants like it. These are kitchens rich in history, steeped in tradition, committed to serving the best food for the benefit of all people. I feel passionately about them and want to support them in any way I can.

I've brought many of my chefs and members of my team here. I want them to experience the roots of our traditions, and the ingredients and techniques that inspire our cooking back in London. I want them to witness the personality, ethos, ethics and attributes of these mothers of Peruvian cooking. It is the closest thing I can do to bottling that spirit and expertise and bringing it back to London.

That day, as I watched Gladys and Ruth in their kitchen, they told me that I was sitting in the very place that had played host to thousands of other customers. Among those visitors was the great Latin American poet Pablo Neruda. Enriched by his experience, inspired and full of love, he looked over the small valley towards the fields of onions and wrote the *Ode to the Onion*, a small tribute to a great region held up by its Andina women.

CAJAMARCA

My uncle and godfather 'Chermo' Morales was stationed in Cajamarca while he worked in the police force during the terror of the Shining Path. He knows its every nook and cranny, making him the perfect guide for my culinary adventure there. We drove all night, travelling inland up the mountainous roads from the coastal region of Lambayeque. When we arrived, the sky was bright orange and the sun was saying its last goodbye over the horizon. I felt the altitude mildly, or perhaps it was a combination of hunger and car-sickness – Chermo's driving was speedy and confident, wrapping us tightly around all the hundreds of bends. Nonetheless, I was honoured to spend quality time with him, the warmest of my uncles, and to discover this region that he knows so well.

Although the early settlers were the Wari, the Incas established Cajamarca as a key region in their empire. As a result the city (also called Cajamarca) saw one of the bloodiest battles between the Incas and the Spanish invaders, resulting in the capture and murder of the Inca Emperor Atahualpa.

Atahualpa ruled Quito in Ecuador between 1525 and 1533, while his brother Huascar ruled the Inca Empire in Peru. The two brothers, though, were locked in a bitter feud that ended in battle and Huascar's death. Atahualpa, victorious, sent his generals to occupy Cusco, while he stayed in Cajamarca. While he was there, the Spanish invader Francisco Pizarro entered the city on the premise of converting the Incas to Christianity. He summoned Atahualpa to a meeting in the main square. Atahualpa made a grand entrance accompanied by 6,000 ceremonial soldiers. Pizarro's men gave Atahualpa a small book of scriptures and a ring as a religious gesture. In seeing no significance in the gifts, Atahualpa threw them to the ground. The Spanish were furious. Immediately, from their hiding places around the square, they opened fire. Mostly unarmed, the Incas could put up little defence and more than 5,000 of them were killed. On Pizarro's order Atahualpa himself was captured. Reports suggest that no Spanish soldiers lost their lives.

Pizarro took Atahualpa hostage in a room that is now known as 'The Rescue Room'. It is 11.8m long, 7.3m wide and 3.1m high. Here, knowing that Pizarro was looking for wealth rather than blood, Atahualpa offered his captors a ransom in exchange for freedom. To this day this remains the biggest ransom ever paid: he promised to have The Rescue Room filled once with gold and twice with silver 'until wherever your hand reaches in height'. In today's money experts suggest that this would equate to a sum greater than half a billion US dollars. The Spaniards accepted, and from all corners of the Inca Empire, the riches of the ransom came to Cajamarca.

However, the Spaniards broke their word, tricked Atahualpa and set up what was essentially a kangaroo court – the trial was a fake and Atahualpa's fate was already sealed. The Spaniards tried him and killed him. This story changed the course of history for western South America: Atahualpa's meeting with the Spanish and his subsequent defeat and death is considered the foundation stone of the ensuing Spanish conquest.

In 1986 Cajamarca was designated a site of Historical and Cultural Heritage. One of the oldest cities in South America, it is today a living celebration of Spanish colonial architecture, beautiful landscapes, pre-Hispanic archeological sites and hot springs. Its gastronomy is as rich as its history. Well known for its dairy produce, its cheeses are spectacular, featuring in many dishes, including the delicious Caldo Verde (p.154), or green soup. As with many Andina soups, this one is packed with vitamins, making it perfect for local workers, who pick up hearty and sustaining bowls at the markets.

A block away from the Plaza de Armas (the main square) and housed in what is a 200-year-old building is a buzzing market packed with stalls selling everything from swimsuits to hats, combs to t-shirts and spring onions to cows' feet. Here, at a stall selling soups and stews, Chermo and I sat down to a bowl of *caldo verde*. Even before the first sip, this glorious soup catches you with its steamy aromas of Mother Nature, fields and grass. It is a life-affirming smell, soothing and kind, ancient, authentic and natural. In Cajamarca traditionally this soup is made using an ancient herb called *chamqa*, although more readily

available herbs are now more common, and it is these that feature in our recipe. The semi-melted cow's milk cheese stirred into the soup is an essential component – it feels like a comforting duvet from within the hot broth. Between the two – the ancient herbs and the cheese – this soup is the perfect marriage of Andina and European cultures.

Of course, there are lots of other dishes to try in Cajamarca's markets. Among them, corn with cheese, *tamales*, *humitas*, wild mushroom ceviche, fried guinea pig with chilli potato, and pumpkin dessert. After the green soup, though, my favourite is the Caldo de Cabeza (p.162) or lamb's head soup. 'Martincito, you have to try this lamb's head soup, it's really good!' shouted Chermo. I did and for a second time stood still. Wow. In Peru, this soup is said to wake the dead. In contrast to the light broth of *caldo verde*, *caldo de cabeza* is thick and rich. It is serious nose-to-tail eating at its finest. The wealth of flavours that come from stewing a lamb's head are worth discovering. A few months after my trip I debuted this dish at home, full head and all, and my fearless kids loved it.

I love my godfather Chermo and I have many wonderful memories of my time in Cajamarca with him. However, the enduring aromas and flavours of the dishes I shared with him there – and the conversations we had about them – are what I remember the most. In a way, the soups and stews we tried in Cajamarca gave us a better insight into people's lives and the history of Cajamarca than even our visit to The Rescue Room. The flavours and textures took us not only to the moment, but also to times way, way back.

AYACUCHO

The dish Puka Picante (p.92) represents the blood that flows in Ayacucho. Its name comes from Quechua *puka*, meaning 'red' and *picante*, denoting a rich spicy stew. Its bright red colour is the result of the native *ayrampo* red berries, beetroot, and panca chillies, which are its main ingredients.

Ayacucho's history is devastating, full of pain, suffering and violence. For some, then, *puka picante* represents the blood unfairly spilled on Ayacucho's land. From the gruesome Battle of Ayacucho that secured independence not only for Peru, but for the whole of South America, to the brutality of the Shining Path, and the ensuing civil war, this is a place that has seen more than its fair share of bloodshed.

Puka picante is said to originate from pre-Inca times. Some say that it was eaten at the funerals of young children, with the pork within the vegetable stew said to represent the bodies of the dead. It was offered in particular to strengthen the fathers who had lost their sons. To me, this sounds a morbid beginning for such a flavourful and colourful dish, one that today brings people together, re-connecting Ayacuchanos with their roots and their lost traditions. It is one of the most poignant, celebrated and influential Andina dishes of all.

In the 1980s and 90s, more than 70,000 people died during the bloody fighting in Peru between the military and the Shining Path. Torture, mutilation and disappearances were common. In the rural parts of the Ayacucho region especially, thousands of humble, innocent local farmers were caught up in the crossfire. This generated a sense of wrath and displacement. Territorial conflict forced locals out of their homes resulting in mass migration from the countryside into the main cities – Ayacucho city itself and then ultimately Lima. Abandoned in their villages, those who survived lost everything, including their communities, their families, their dignity, their roots and even their traditions. In every corner of the Ayacucho region, the physical and emotional scars of war are still evident even today. That said, like so many tortured regions of Peru, in Ayacucho there is hope. I see it in local tradition and creativity, and in particular in the wonderful, bright red dish of *puka picante*.

I had waited all my life to visit Ayacucho – and finally I made it in 2016. As a child, I'd feared the place. Like Berlin in the mid-40s, Saigon in the late-60s, Fallujah in the mid-2000s and Aleppo today, Ayacucho in the 90s was a place of deep, unpredictable conflict. During the first few years of terrorist attacks in Peru, when I was around ten years old and living in Lima, newsreels told of how the majority of the fighting was in Ayacucho. For me, then, this place came to represent everything that was fear and terror, especially once the Shining Path had threatened my father and I'd come home one day to find armed guards at my house. In fact, they were there to protect us – but for my ten-year-old self the mere sight of them felt like being strangled.

I had spent the previous 24 hours listening to bombs go off, and watching news reports about the brutal advances of the Shining Path and their acts of atrocity against the communities living in the Andes – and in particular in Ayacucho, the headquarters of the insurrection. To me, then, Ayacucho was a region to fear most. It is a bitter prophecy that the word *ayacucho* itself means 'the corner of death'.

Still, I believe that the only way to exorcise your demons is to confront them, so in 2016 I decided to visit. I hoped to find peace and reconstruction in all aspects of life there.

And so I did. Ayacucho today is a beautiful place. Actually, it is more than beautiful: it is a treasure. In the city (named Ayacucho, like the region), the gorgeous main square is a colonial masterpiece. Throughout, the city is peppered with more than 33 churches that boast some of the finest architecture in the Andes. At night, it is all lit up, elegant and dazzling, showing itself off in all its glory. I discovered a people whose faith and religious customs are exemplary among the Andina communities. Over Easter and the Holy Week, Ayacucho's ten-day celebrations are considered the most important in Latin America and even among the biggest in the world. Thousands of Peruvians and tourists arrive

in the city to participate in the ceremonies and processions, and to experience the cultural, artistic and gastronomic delights.

Ayacucho's cuisine is a Pandora's box characterized by rich flavours and wide variety. Dishes and drinks such as not only *puka picante*, but also Pachamanca (p.109), El Puchero (p.167), Humitas (p.187), Ponche (p.194) and Chicha (p.199), among others, are served up both in markets and in homes, but they are also important traditional fare that form part of the feasting during celebrations and festivities.

Most of the region lies in the mountains of the Andes, some in the jungle, and agriculture and livestock provide the main sources of income for the region's economy. In the jungle the dominant crops are cocoa and coffee, grown mainly for the international market; while in the mountains the region gives us potatoes, corn, barley, wheat and *olluco*. Especially important is the grain quinoa, which has given its name to one of the region's most significant towns, Quinua, in Huamanga province.

When I visited I made a trip to the quinoa fields of the organic farmers we work with there, and saw the way our quinoa is processed. I went to the monument on the road to Quinua up on the Pampa de Ayacucho, an obelisk erected to commemorate those who lost their lives in the Battle of Ayacucho and helped to secure independence for Peru. The town of Quinua itself brims with wonderful, creative artisan potters. Ayacucho has a reputation as Peru's capital of arts and crafts. Textiles, wood- and stone-carving, tin-sculpting and more than 55 other artistic crafts are at home here. And it is not just physical art for which Ayacucho is famous: in my previous life I was a music producer. Some 15 years ago, long before I visited Ayacucho itself, I had the chance to meet the master of Andina blues, Raúl García Zárate, who comes from the region.

A highlight for me during any of my regional adventures is always a visit to the local food markets. Two blocks away from Ayacucho's main square is Carlos F. Vivanco Market. More than 108 years old, the market is a bustling place with plentiful ingredients and delicacies to taste on every corner.

I made the most of my time, joyfully eating my way through the stalls, as well as commissioning crafts and artwork for our restaurants. But, my most memorable time during my visit was an excursion to the Museo de la Memoria (Museum of the Memory). Through photos, videos, clothing and re-enactment, this incredible museum shares myriad personal stories that pay homage to all those who lost their lives during the armed conflict. Not only did it feel like a place of bravery, but also a place that laid bare the sacrifice and anger of the Ayacucho people. My feeling was compounded by the group of a dozen or so women I encountered when I arrived. Aged in their sixties and dressed in traditional dress, they stopped me in my tracks. 'Do you meet here often?' I asked them. With a sad look one of them said to me, 'Yes. Every single week. We meet to organize our appeal to the authorities to give us the bodies of our husbands.' Theirs is a story told across the whole of this region. They are widows whose husbands disappeared in the fighting. Now they are undertaking their own fight – for information and for the right to have their husbands' bodies recovered and laid to rest.

After I left the museum and for the next few days, I kept seeing groups of women in their sixties walking the streets. I also saw many on their own. It didn't take me long to realize that Ayacucho is a region with far more women than men; and that almost every woman over the age of 55 in Ayacucho is probably a widow.

Yet, at the same time, and even though when I think about what has happened in the region I am deeply angered, today I see a supportive community that is taking the path of progress. For every sad story I heard during my visit, I found a story of inspiration and strength; for every shattered memory, I also heard many colourful dreams. Overall, in the city, in the villages and in the people, there is a sense of peace. There is a long way to go to repair and compensate the region for its innumerable, unbearable losses, but I feel that its people are getting their lives back. This enduring spirit is what draws me to stand tall with the people of Ayacucho; it is what finally gives me the strength to let go of my own fear.

If you ever intend to visit Peru, I encourage you to seek out this magical place. Even from home find out about it, fight for it, help it to prosper again. In our own small way, to pay homage to Ayacucho, at Casita Andina we serve *puka picante*. Just in case anyone is superstitious (remember the significance of the pieces of pork), our version is vegetarian. Our chef Vito created it this way to give our customers, as he put it, 'a sexy dish'. I think it is also an excuse to tell our customers an old Ayacucho saying: '*Que te demores en partir y que te apures en volver*', meaning 'May you take a long while to leave, but hurry up in coming back.' It is a dish that is best eaten slowly and savoured. Then, once you've tried it once, you will come running back for more.

Finally, at the entrance in the back of Casita Andina you will find a beautifully hand-embroidered postcard made by Doña Leonila Ore. I bought it from the Museum of the Memory. Doña Leonila and many other widows make these postcards to raise funds to continue the mission to find out what happened to their husbands and other relatives. For me, it is a symbol of their struggle, strength and hope, and a reminder to me to be grateful for my heritage, my ancestors and most of all my family.

PUNO

The region of Puno is located in the southeast of Peru. It borders with Bolivia to the east, Cusco and Arequipa to the west, Moquegua and Tacna to the south and Madre de Dios, the Amazonian region, to the north. At 3,800m above sea level, Puno city, its capital, is one of the highest cities in Peru.

The region has strong roots in Quechua and Aymara cultures, the latter of which harks back to the Tiahuanaco, who reigned there as early as 1000CE. In the 15th century the Incas took over, then the Spanish conquistadors, who flocked to the region in search of minerals. However, despite the wealth that lies in Puno's soils, it is folklore for which Puno is most well known. Home to more than 100 varieties of traditional dance, Puno gives us the famous Diablada, the 'devil dance' performed during the Festivity of the Virgin of the Candelaria of Puno, a UNESCO-accredited celebration that takes place during the first two weeks of February. Hundreds of visitors come from all over Peru, as well as from abroad, making it one of the most important religious events in Latin America.

For a long time Puno's gastronomy was the stuff of legend for me. I'd long heard about a succulent roast lamb, known by the traditional name of *kankacho*, that was the work of a certain Doña Julia Luna from the village of Ayaviri. Having been marinated in a blend of panca chilli, garlic and lager, the tender male lamb's leg was then slow-cooked for seven hours in a wood-fired oven. And if the lamb wasn't enough to tempt me, the British writer and geologist David Forbes wrote in his book *On The Aymara Indians of Bolivia and Peru* (1870) that the '*chairo* has at first a far from inviting aspect, which certainly would not recommend it at a European table, a taste for it is soon acquired, and it is even relished by the traveller who visits the inhospitable Puna of Bolivia and Peru'. Put simply, Chairo (p.165) might not be the most attractive soup in the world, but its flavours are second to none. It is the ugly duckling of the soup world; the Cinderella, who, dressed in rags, hides a fundamental, irresistible beauty.

I've had the pleasure of having *chairo* several times in the city of Puno. This is a bustling place, a frontier town between Peru and Bolivia, on the shores of Lake Titicaca, the highest lake in the world. When I visited, as I approached Puno, I couldn't make out the lake from the sky. As is my instinct, though, I searched out Puno's central market. Among the throng, I spotted a busy *chairo* soup-seller. With a large pot, almost as big as the seller herself, she stirred her soup and offered it to her customers, who came to sit in small benches right up close to her. I felt completely at home huddled up around this seller and her massive pot. In part it was the immediacy and quick service, a spontaneity that I seek to replicate at our restaurants in London; but also I felt at home in the pride in the soup-seller's face. She had utter confidence in her ability to offer great seasoning and great flavours in her dish. There was no fusion, no blending; it was truly authentic. Why? Because *chairo* is basic and practical; the quintessential Andina soup. It uses what is local and readily available. This is an organic, low-cost, zero-waste, zero-carbon-footprint soup.

The word *chairo* comes from both the Aymara and the Quechua languages and it means 'food' or 'bag of food'. Traditionally, it was made for peasant farmers to provide energy for a whole day's work. Thick and nutritionally dense, it gave sustenance to the men working far from home each day. Underneath the murky façade of browns, greys and sometimes even black colours (the result of the black *chuño* – freeze-dried black potatoes – in it), the soup has deep, rewarding flavours. It is a symbol of strength, not only for those working the land, but also against conquistadors and dictators – like the Andinas and Andinos themselves, it has endured for more than a thousand years.

The region of Puno is a powerhouse of soup production, and no wonder at such high altitudes with a cold climate, but *chairo* finds variations elsewhere in the Andes, too. In neighbouring Arequipa it is spiced with chilli, giving it a slightly reddish colour; in Apurímac it is whiter, usually made using white freeze-dried potatoes, rather than black ones.

Puno is also the centre of Peru's quinoa farming. Since before the Incas, quinoa has been prized more than gold. With quinoa featuring so extensively on our restaurant menus, I have travelled throughout the Andes making it my business to understand about the different types and how to plant, harvest and use each one. Quinoa is gluten-free, has twice the protein content of barley or rice, and is also rich in magnesium, calcium, iron, zinc, vitamins B and E and dietary fibre. It is so nutritious that UN declared 2013 the Year of Quinoa, in the hope it may be used to help eradicate hunger and malnutrition the world over.

All this has had economic implications for rural quinoa farmers. So, as well as learning about the grain itself, I have wanted to understand how the global explosion of quinoa's popularity has affected the Andina farming communities. Even before 2013, Peru's quinoa farmers had begun to export massive quantities of their grain internationally. What has struck me most has been the overall prosperity that has been realized as a result of the increased distribution chain: farmers have had regular work and a reliable and growing income.

By 2014, as a result of the UN initiative, demand for quinoa had grown to its highest in recorded history. While the crop for a year or so became somewhat more scarce and so more expensive for the locals themselves, they had plentiful access to amaranth and many other nutritious alternative ingredients to ensure their own continued balanced diet. Media reports at the time issued scaremongering: that the effects on the local farmers were malnutrition and poverty. This isn't true. The growth in demand for quinoa has been beneficial for Andina farmers. My own visit to Puno was a brilliant reminder of how important this grain is both to our dishes and to the Andina economy. I have included in this book a straightforward seasoned Pesque de Quinua (p.144) with cheese, just like the one I tasted in Puno, because I think this is the simplest quinoa recipe of all.

I've also featured a Puno-inspired recipe for Sango (p.138). Before Chinese settlers brought rice to Peru, and even well before the arrival of the Spanish, the staples were potatoes, tubers and *sango*. An ancient dish, the name originates from the Quechua word *sanku* meaning 'corn dough'. Over time, *sango* has become an accompaniment to both savoury stews and sweet desserts. By the 19th century, it had found its way down the mountains to the coast and had become a popular dessert for the street vendors in Lima. My recipe brings it together with Adobo de Pato, a succulent duck stew with roots in Arequipa – a perfect fusion of two of the Andina regions' native ingredients.

Traditional Aymara cooking from Puno uses a lot of offal. For this reason I've also given you Picante de Lengua (p.146), an ox-tongue stew. Peasant food it may be, but this dish is one of the most flavour-packed of the Peruvian Andes. Try it, and remember, like with the *chairo*, the beauty lies within.

HUÁNUCO

An auntie once told me that my Great Aunt Carmela had dated the son of the Huánuco-born composer Daniel Alomía Robles, who wrote the famous song *El Cóndor Pasa* in 1913. More than 4,000 versions of this song now exist, including the version by Simon & Garfunkel. I've known about the story of our family's connection to *El Cóndor Pasa* for many years, and its composer and Huánuco have always intrigued me.

Huánuco is the place where the oldest human remains have been found in Peru. Its roots are in the indigenous Lauricocha culture, which dates back 9,000 years, but it has also been home to the Yaros, and became an area of great importance for the Incas. Huánuco's territory covers both mountain and jungle. It has important water resources thanks to its many rivers, lagoons and breathtaking lakes, as well as some of the highest mountains in Peru. Its steep jungle terrain attracts many visitors.

With diverse geography naturally comes a diverse climate. The jungle is warm and humid; the mountains are cold and clear. As a result the region also produces many different crops: a host of tubers, corn, wheat, fruits and vegetables, as well as bananas and coffee. However, in Huánuco it is the potato that is king: here, Peru's three key potato varieties – *amarilla*, *yungay* and *huayro* – grow in abundance. In fact, Huánuco produces more of them combined than any other region in Peru.

The most typical ingredient of Huánuco is the herb *chincho*. Mint-like, it is easy and quick to grow and gives personality to many of the region's key dishes, including the distinctive pork *pachamanca*. Traditionally cooked using hot stones, Pachamanca (p.109) is the most ancestral of all our Andina dishes, appearing throughout the Andes in various forms. Each region adds its own characteristic flavours (in this case of *chincho*), marinating the meats with local herbs or chillies, and adding locally grown ingredients to complete the dish. Another favourite is called Tacacho (p.96), from a Quechua word meaning 'to smash'. This is plantain that has been cooked, then mashed, seasoned and made into spheres or small patties. A representative dish from the jungle area of Huánuco, it appears in various forms all over the Amazon; the version in this book is a fusion one that we love and is fun to make.

My other favourite, Chaufa (p.108), from the Cantonese word *chau fan*, meaning 'to flambée or fry rice', fascinates me because it represents a significant culinary and cultural influence that exists in the Peruvian Andes – and one that some might say is unexpected. In the 1850s, Chinese immigrants arrived in Peru looking for work and a better life. They settled in places such as Huánuco, working in agriculture or as hired help on the plantations. In 1952, residents of Huánuco with Chinese ancestry set up the Chun Wa Association. The organization aimed to promote the principles and moral code for a good life valued in China itself in order to provide support for the community. The association survives today, fervently observing many Chinese traditions and ceremonies, including Chinese New Year.

There is no single, representative *chaufa* rice recipe, so I have given myself licence to propose a contemporary take on it, using tempeh. After all, any dish adopted by one culture from another evolves to include local, seasonal ingredients. Like the 4,000 variations of *El Cóndor Pasa*, one dish can become many dishes, each with its own place in the world.

CUSCO

My first ever flight over the Andes en route to Cusco was spectacular. The skies were crystal clear, shafts of sunlight hit the highlands below and, as we neared our destination, I watched the beautiful snowcapped peaks appear so close that they almost tickled the belly of the plane. From that altitude you can see the way in which agriculture shapes and moulds the landscape. Colourful fields of potato, corn, quinoa and beans of all kinds spread out across the different heights. The many lush shades made the whole landscape look like an unsolved Rubik's cube. At times you can see majestic village churches, steeples pointing upwards and painted in bright blues or yellows. Occasionally, when I looked down I could see people gathered, and I knew this would be a food market. The mere thought of those culinary treasure-troves gives me goosebumps even now.

I first went to Cusco when I was 14 years old – it formed part of my first trip back to Peru after moving to England and the first time I had seen my mother in three years. I had missed her terribly, and she had missed me – she wanted to mark our reunion not with a stay in Lima, where she lived, but with an adventure. We were to start that adventure straightaway – in Cusco, one of the highest regions in Peru.

With so little time to acclimatize, it was hardly surprising that when we arrived in Cusco city (like so many places in Peru, one name is given to both the region and its capital), I was overcome with altitude sickness. But my mother has tireless energy – some say that's where I get it from – and before I could think about it we were driving to Sacsayhuaman, a citadel on the outskirts of Cusco city, then for a few hours on to Pisac, with its world-famous artisan craft market, and then to the Inca ruins at Ollantaytambo. It was a lot for one day, and it meant that I had no choice but to acclimatize quickly. It also meant that by the second day, I was fit enough to carry on happily to Machu Picchu, the 'lost city of the Incas' and one of the most impressive places to visit on Earth. My most vivid memories, though, are of several delicious ingredients and dishes we had along the way. And I'll never forget the incredible papaya jam we had every morning at our hotel.

I now go to Cusco regularly to visit the charity project, called Amantani, I work with, and to look for new ingredients, producers and culinary inspiration. For me, the region is a chef's paradise; its gastronomy, like its architecture, is one of the greatest expressions of the Inca Empire's most impressive achievements.

Located in the south of the Peruvian Andes, the city of Cusco is in a fertile valley that lies 3,400m above sea level. The name Cusco comes from the Quechua word *qosqo*, which literally translated means 'belly button' – making Cusco the belly button (or centre) of South America. Founded by the Inca Manco Cápac in the 12th century, and later expanded and ruled by Pachacutec, Cusco became the capital of the Tahuantinsuyo – the Inca Empire and the largest pre-Columbian empire in the Americas. Cusco was where the administrative, political and military decisions of the Empire took place.

In the Inca Empire everything was managed through the *ayllu* system in which the ownership of livestock, land and water was the right of all those who lived in the village, as long as the inhabitants followed the established rules. Communal work on the land, including planting and harvesting, occurred alongside the building of roads, bridges and buildings, and even military service. The advanced agricultural techniques included aqueducts, and water channels for irrigation, known as *andenes*, which exist to this day. *Andenes* are stepped, levelled platforms hewn into the sides of the mountains and they enabled Inca farmers, and farmers since, to grow plentiful crops on small plots of land. The agricultural calender was established by the apparent path of the sun and moon across the sky, giving 12 months each of 30 days. Livestock, including cattle, llama, ducks and guinea pigs, and indigenous ingredients, such as potato, corn, quinoa and chillies, all flourish there, and are bought and sold using the traditional system of barter known as *el trueque*.

On my last visit to Cusco, I headed straight for the Urubamba Valley where the altitude is lower than that in Cusco city – I had learnt my lesson on the trip with my mother. In further contrast to that early adventure, on my first day I did nothing but take in the views, eat light meals and drink coca tea (p.194) to settle my stomach. The people of the Andes have been consuming coca for more than 4,000 years. The Incas saw this native ingredient as a generous gift of friendship from the gods, and today it is the usual way to welcome visitors to the region.

The hotel where I stayed has a ten-acre organic plantation where I could search for ingredients and use them to cook for myself. One of the dishes I wanted to create was Kapchi de Setas (p.152), a favourite of mine. This winter dish is made primarily using wild mushrooms, gathered from the local forests where they grow abundantly after rainfall. It was a joy to make it in the Urubamba Valley, where it has been made for thousands of years. There is something deeply harmonious about using ingredients provided by Mother Nature in a place and at a time that she intended. How I felt then must have been how the Incas felt, cooking with the seasons from the land around them every day. No wonder they worshipped Pachamama – Mother Earth, the provider.

Cusco is home to San Pedro Market, one of my favourite markets in the world. It is aisle after aisle of treasure, each row carefully organized by its theme. Breadmakers from the regional town of Oropesa come to sell their *chuta* (a kind of flat bread). The cheesemakers, with their beautiful displays, offer samples of cow's and goat's milk cheeses. Fruit and vegetable sellers, based right in the middle of the market, layer up their glorious fresh produce in stacks that defy gravity. And butchers cut their meat with great pride, in front of your eyes, offering up every part of the animal for sale in line with the nose-to-tail eating of Andina food philosophy.

My favourite aisle, though, is what I call the 'Fruit Juice Army' aisle. Here, the sellers – all women, all glamorous – wear beautifully ironed uniforms of colourful bibs, immaculate surgical-white aprons and neatly lopsided hats. They mix up juices and smoothies using everything from well-known fruits to medicinal herbs and nutritious grains as well as dark beer and herbal teas. The last time I visited, each of the thirty or so Fruit Juice Army ladies was sitting

atop a throne of fresh fruit. Customers in Peru are very demanding – we can taste something that is not ripe or fresh, and we don't accept pre-prepared ingredients. For the sellers, then, there are no compromises. Once you place your order, drink-making is meticulous, energetic and fast. Everything is freshly cut, mixed and blended in front of your eyes. On that day I had a delicious mix of cooked local white quinoa with lucuma, peach, mango and milk – the perfect energizer for my day ahead.

When I choose somewhere to eat, I always veer towards stalls that have dishes I've never tried or that provide local, traditional food. That day I decided on a stall where an elderly lady sat in full traditional dress and holding a baby lamb. This was her regular lunch spot when she came to sell produce in the market – not the lamb I might add, that was her pet. She introduced me to the stall-owners, who reminded me of my great aunts Carmela and Otilia and were serving up traditional dishes such as pork *chicharrón* with mote corn, pork *adobo* stew with rice, and my favourite Olluquito con Charqui (p.104). It is said that this is one of the oldest dishes in the Andes, dating back some 4,500 years, and was popular with the Inca emperors. It is made using *olluco* tubers and an alpaca jerky and each ingredient seems to me highly representative of Cusco's vast history. I take just a few mouthfuls and relish in its flavours. My friend and her little lamb, who got to try morsels of it, too, also seemed to be relishing this dish. In one way I felt envious of them: this was their routine, every day they could have access to this wonderful food in a way that I never could. In another way, though, I knew that if I could put this Cusco wonder in my book, I would be connecting my two worlds. I could be grateful not just for Cusco, the Empire and its great culinary treats, but for Mother Earth herself.

APURÍMAC

In 2009, after having worked for almost 18 years in the music business, I decided to change my life and start over. I had a dream to create the most beautiful Peruvian restaurant in London. My burning desire to cook the food of my country became an obsession, leading me down a road that, little did I know, would be the most challenging in my life. Once I'd made the commitment, over and over in my head the one phrase that I used to motivate me was '*El timbre del éxito consiste en lanzarse a la profundidad sin perder la cabeza nunca.*' Or, 'The sound of success consists in throwing yourself into the depths without losing your head.'

It was the great Apurímac writer and anthropologist José María Arguedas who first uttered these words. Known as the leading light in the indigenous literature movement of Peru, Arguedas suffered greatly through his early childhood. He was displaced through neglect and poverty many times, finding release only through his research, work and writings. Tragically, aged 58, he put a gun to his head, ending not only his life but the painful depression he had suffered for more than a decade. As a child I had heard of Arguedas, but it was not until I went to university in Leeds that my brilliant Peruvian lecturer Roberto Rodriguez gave me a copy of *Yawar Fiesta* – Arguedas' second novel – to study. Arguedas painted images in my head and connected the dots in my indigenous ancestry. As a displaced and migrant child myself, I related to his story, and along the way I also learnt a lot about Peruvian culture and about the beauty, frustrations and hardship in the Apurímac region.

Apurímac is also the birthplace of my friend and chef Richard Llacta, who worked with us in London for a few years, before heading off to follow his own dreams. I think he liked me because his grandfather, who had taken care of him as a child, was also called Martin. He grew up in Vito, a village in Apurímac that until recently had no roads, electricity, water or sewage and was accessible only

by horse. As a child, he and his friends played football until sunset. Without a watch to tell them when it was teatime, they knew it was time to go home only when the sun no longer shone on the mountaintop. Richard has described Vito as a place forgotten by God. However, in Quechua the word Apurímac means 'where the gods speak', *apu* meaning 'lord' and the revered mountains representing the seat of the gods, from where they offer advice and guidance to the people. For the Incas, the Apurímac mountains were a place of reverence.

Located in south–central Peru, Apurímac is the smallest Andina region. In fact, it is named after the river that flows through it and is served by deep valleys and canyons, and wild peaks in a highland that reaches almost 4,000m. Before the Incas arrived, the Chancas, the rebellious and fearless warriors of ancient Peru, lived here. They were great farmers, too, and for thousands of years cultivated many of the Andes' wonderful ingredients.

A home to puma, spectacled bears, wild deer, birds and fish of many species, the region provides habitats at many different altitudes, each with its own climate. Archaeologists have discovered that the diet and cooking techniques (over a wood-burning stove) of the people of Apurímac thousands of years ago was not much different to that of today. My favourite ingredient known here is probably the *cushuro*. Found growing wild on rocks near lagoons, these curious little balls are a soft and squidgy bacteria, sometimes nicknamed Andina caviar. Ranging in diameter from 3mm to 40mm, the colour of each ball may vary from green to reddish brown. The balls are high in calcium, phosphorus, iron and a variety of B-vitamins, and they are also very beautiful – adding pearls to any dish. You'll find them in soups and ceviches, as well as in stews.

More than 400 varieties of potato are said to grow in Apurímac alongside *mashua* (a root vegetable), corn, barley, physalis, sugar cane, coffee, beans, pulses, amaranth and avocados. In Apurímac, the cuisine is distinctive for its use of aromatic herbs, such as *muña*, mint, *paico* and parsley, and its native vegetables, many of which grow wild – *ataqo*, *lavano*, *llullucha* and *murmunta* among them.

There are many specific Apurímac dishes that I love, but my favourite is Yawar Picante (p.28). The name comes from the Quechua words meaning 'blood stew' and the dish is a typical representation of Andina nose-to-tail eating. Made using blood and offal, *yawar picante* is sometimes formed into a sausage, rather as you might find black pudding or morcilla. At other times, though, its ingredients are cooked loosely, as in the recipe in this book.

Andina cooking crosses borders and boundaries and the Kapchi de Setas (p.152) – a delicious wild mushroom soup, and Chochoca (p.164) that my aunts brought to Lima from their home in La Libertad also form part of the Apurímac gastronomic repertoire. Apurímac is also known for its *ponches* (p.194), festival and celebration drinks that might include fruits or spices, be served hot or cold, and with or without alcohol. I think if I were an Apurímeño, I'd want the strong version, as this land is tough and rugged and its mountain gods have been silent for a long time.

If I could have any launch party for my book, it would be here in the mountains of Apurímac. I would invite José María Arguedas and my friend Richard and I would listen to their stories of this land. We would drink much oomphed-up *ponche* and to end the night we would all shout the immortal Quechua words, made famous by Arguedas himself, '*Kachkaniraqmi*!' – 'We carry on being!'

PASCO

On 28th July 1904, a man named Victor Vaughan Morris, from Utah, was leading the preparations for the inauguration of the train line that travelled from the port of Callao to the then phenomenally prosperous Andina mining town of Cerro de Pasco, Pasco's capital city, high up in the Andes. The place had become home to the world's greatest copper mine. Filled with dreams of wealth and glory, Victor had come to the Andes to work for the Cerro de Pasco Mining Company, which had not only bought the rights to mine, but also to build the train line. Victor began working in the sales department of the train company. Soon, he was Director, and by the time of the inaugural train journey, he was fully in charge.

The day of the inauguration was also Peru's National Independence Day. Some 5,000 people were gathered, among them distinguished guests from the USA and from government and high society in Peru. Victor was in charge of the celebration, including the drinks. Without any whiskey on hand to make the classic whiskey sour, he used Peru's national spirit, pisco, instead. The Pisco Sour was born.

Pasco and its towns and cities have always intrigued me. Not only because it was the birthplace of Peru's national cocktail, but also because my father worked for the Cerro de Pasco Mining Company when he first arrived in Peru in the 1960s.

Located right in the centre of Peru, although sections of Pasco lie within the Andes, mostly the region is Amazonian. Overall, then, it is the smallest Andina region, and yet it still manages to play host to mountains, lakes, glaciers, valleys, and archaeological sites of great importance. Throughout Peru's history, Pasco has played a crucial part in the struggle for progress. Its history is turbulent, unjust and even at times catastrophic, but it is also triumphant.

At 4,330m above sea level, Cerro de Pasco is one of the highest cities in the world. During the city's heyday mining brought wealth and prosperity, securing Cerro de Pasco as an important economic centre for Peru. However, with highs come lows and years of exploitation have not only harmed the city's landscape and infrastructure, but also its people. There is devastating pollution: at the centre lies an open mine – a crater that leaks toxins into the atmosphere. Furthermore, drug lords use pockets of land to farm coca for cocaine.

The harsh weather and altitude cause their own hardships for the people of Pasco, but still many ancient and native ingredients thrive here. These form the basis of some of Pasco's oldest dishes (some of which occur elsewhere too, of course), including Pachamanca (p.109), Caldo Verde (p.154), Caldo de Cabeza (p.162), and the capital's representative dish *charquicán*, which is a little like our Olluquito con Charqui (p.104) except mushier. Made with potatoes, tubers, chilli, dried llama or alpaca meat, and maca root, this nutritious dish was said to fortify soldiers who fought the War of Independence back in the 19th century.

Pasco is one of the most diverse regions in Peru in terms of ethnicity and language. A variety of indigenous cultures settled there thousands of years ago, then in the 16th century the Spanish conquistadors arrived. Americans came to find wealth during the mining years, followed by, among others, northern Europeans who came from artistic and farming communities. In fact, Pasco now counts among its peoples not only those with indigenous roots and *mestizos* (people of combined descent), but also those with Spanish, Italian, African, Asian, German and Austrian ancestry.

In the late-1800s the Germans and Austrians founded Oxapampa, in eastern Pasco. As a result of poor infrastructure and lack of access, for 50 years or more they lived in almost total isolation, incubating their traditions, dances, music and gastronomy. Today, a mixture of native and non-native ingredients grow here, including *olluco, oca*, rice, corn, beans, cassava, banana, oranges, papaya, chillies and coffee. Villa Rica in Pasco is known as the coffee capital of Peru, and Oxapampa and nearby Pozuzo (also populated mainly by descendants from Germany and Austria) are gaining a reputation for livestock farming, including excellent beef, pork and lamb, as well as cured meats, honey, and milk products. All manner of fruit orchards provide the ingredients for increasingly sought-after jams and marmalades. One of my favourite fusion dishes from the region is Shtrukala (p.190), which is a take on a strudel, made with banana.

Despite any hardship, and no matter which melting pot of cultures has come together, Pasco is a region filled with festivity and dancing. In May, Pasco celebrates La Fiesta de las Cruces (the Festival of the Cross), during which the locals participate in colourful dances, all against the backdrop of traditional festival food and drink.

In fact, as far as drinks are concerned, today you will rarely find a Pisco Sour in Pasco itself. Instead, ancient Chicha (p.199) and the sugarcane liquor *guarapo* are more likely to pass your lips – both are firm favourites at the many regional events. But if you're determined, while you might need to visit Lima (or Andina in London) to sip a pisco sour from a bar menu, I feel sure that if you visited the train station in Cerro de Pasco, you would find someone quietly saying '*Salud!*' and raising a glass at the very spot of the birth of our country's world-famous cocktail.

JUNÍN

The rugged terrain of Junín covers two ecosystems, those of the Andes and the Amazon. In the southwest, Andina part of Junín, in the valley of the Mantaro River, the weather is mild and dry, providing the perfect conditions for potato, corn, green peas, carrots and broad beans. The warm, humid jungle, meanwhile, makes Junín the number-one orange producer in the country. This area also gives us pineapple, clementines and bananas, and yuca, coffee and cacao.

The capital of Junín is Huancayo, the most important city in the central Andes. Huancayo as we know it today was founded in 1572, but its history dates back to around 1200BCE, when it was inhabited by the Huancas. This is the source of some of the finest indigenous ingredients for Andina gastronomic culture. Unsurprisingly, then, it also has its own unique, rich gastronomy. Some of its dishes, such as the Papa a la Huancaína (p.51), have even become standout recipes that represent the whole of Peru.

I was in Huancayo recently, and every time I visit something surprising happens. I left Lima at dawn one rainy and cold morning. The flight takes an hour and a half, soaring over multicoloured fields planted with a variety of crops and scattered with small adobe houses. The airport, at Jauja, is 3,400m above sea level – when you get off the plane the altitude hits you. You have to calm your breathing, making it slow and deliberate. For those not already acclimatized, this is a region that forces you to pace yourself.

One of the best things about Junín is that you have to drive only a few miles before arriving somewhere beautiful, filled with gastronomic treasures. On this trip, before long I came to the main square at the pretty town of Concepción. Here, my guide Dave had recommended Casita Del Lechón (the 'Little House of the Roast Pig'), a food stall run by the very sweet and enthusiastic Doña Carmencita. I was in time to be the first in line. Confident, and smiling from ear to ear, Carmencita revealed what appeared to be a body, all wrapped up in a

blanket and cardboard. She unfolded a corner for me. I was hit with the dizzying aromas of stunning slow-roasted, succulent pork.

Carmencita served me the first portion, and on the side she gave me her homemade llactan sauce (p.47). *'Con un poco de orejita crocante por favor'* ('With a little bit of ear-crackling please'), I asked. I stuffed the meat, crackling and sauce inside freshly baked artisan bread from the stall next door. Munch. Yum. The deep, pork flavours and spicy chilli sauce perked up my taste buds. With that and Carmencita's warm hospitality, wow! I felt a great Huancayo welcome.

Carmencita explained how for six nights a week, she interrupts her sleep so that she can cook, turning the whole pork regularly while it roasts over an open fire, which she tops up with wood every three hours. On those days she finally gets up properly at 6am and rushes to her stall. She has a short nap in the late afternoon, then goes back to doing the same thing again the following night and day. Dave attests to this as he comes here often: 'She is a bit of a hero of mine,' he says. 'Mine, too,' I respond.

Next, I headed for Ingenio, home to one of the oldest and (aptly) most ingenious trout farms in Peru. The farm is built on a steep hillside and harnesses the power of the rapids of the River Chiapuquio to distribute fresh water and fish into large pools. Although many people think rainbow trout are indigenous to the Andes, in fact they are not. Apparently, in 1924 the Peruvian Dr J.R. Mitchell and the English engineer B.T. College, both Cerro de Pasco Mining Corporation employees and fishing enthusiasts, brought fertilized rainbow trout eggs from California and incubated them in a local lake, intending to provide themselves and other fishermen with a place to practise their sport.

Their first attempt at breeding the fish failed, but the next time fifty fish survived and grew to full size. In 1930, they gave their friend Juan Morales Vivanco some fully grown trout – he used them to start a trout farm in Ingenio. Today the farm has 75 pools with around sixty fish in each. It is a model for sustainable farming and is a fascinating tourist attraction. And the fact that trout farming is now such a significant local industry, means that trout dishes such as Trucha a la Parrilla (p.116) are aplenty.

The fish farmers invited me to get involved in the checking, measuring and auditing of the fish in one of the many pools. Kitting me out in waterproof waders, gloves and apron, the fish farmers invited me in. I helped corral the fish into our pool with a wide net, then catch them one by one (see photographs, pp.80–81). Together, the fish farmers and I catalogued each trout, measuring its weight and checking the females for signs of eggs. I have never seen anything like it: the fishermen taught me that if I pressed gently on the back of the female fish, I could squeeze out the eggs almost on demand, catching the roe in my thick, wet glove. '*Comelo*' ('Eat it'), one of them urged. Trout roe is a key ingredient in our Trout Tiradito (p.78) at Casita Andina, so how could I refuse? It was silky smooth, so sweet and juicy. I wished I could gather a portion for my team back in London.

The drive from the fishery towards Huancayo takes you past fields of artichokes – next to fish, artichokes, I think, are the region's most delicious ingredients. On our journey we stopped at a riverside restaurant to taste dishes made using both. Standout was a stunning artichoke ceviche that has inspired the version in this book (p.87).

Food markets are the lifeblood of any town: in Huancayo's markets you can feel the heartbeat in the way sellers interact with their public, from how they display their produce to the noise, discussion and bartering. Stall-holders, who must learn to be hustlers to survive, are packed into halls full of movement and push and shove. These are hectic, forever-changing environments. At Maltería Market in Huancayo, I walked through a hall filled with potatoes and tubers of all varieties. I spotted two *tocosh* sellers. I would have loved to have included a *tocosh* recipe in this book, but it just wasn't practical. *Tocosh* is a white potato that has been fermented using a traditional pre-Inca fermentation technique. To make the *tocosh*, you need to dig a well of about 1m deep on a river bank. You then wrap the potatoes with a mesh, place them inside the well and cover them with heavy stones, which squash the potatoes down. Then, you let the river flow around the potatoes, leaving them where they are for six months. After that time you remove the parcel from the water to reveal a pungent foodstuff that looks (and smells) like overcooked potatoes mixed with blue cheese; bitter but with more natural penicillin than pills made by pharmaceutical companies! Best of all, you can use it to make a great dessert.

I had been told that at Maltería Market, Doña Esther Quispe Rodríguez does the best Gelatina de Pata (p.185) or Foot Jelly. When I first made this dish in the UK, I was met largely with a sense of disgust. But, to me, there is beauty in any recipe that is delicious, nutritious or different; I approach all ingredients with no prejudice whatsoever. Esther looked at me sternly at first: she is used to Limeños turning on their heel once they realize what she uses to make her desserts. I reassured her that I knew about this dish and had made it myself. Impressed, she told me all about her cooking techniques: she slow-cooks cows' feet, extracts the jelly, and adds spices and Demerara sugar. The result is a dessert full of protein that's great for the joints and for skin and tissue replenishment. I tried it: hers has an agreeable sweet and subtle taste, and with such health properties, I can't see why anyone would not want to tuck in.

That night Dave took us to the Instituto Continental, Huancayo's main culinary school, which is where he teaches. One of Dave's colleagues, the chef and teacher Mrs Pamela Rojas, told me about her love for pastry and her work with some of Lima's best bakers. We ended up talking about steamed buns.

'We have traditional steamed buns called *otongo* in Huancayo, too, you know?' she said. Chinese bao buns are a favourite of mine, but I'd never heard about a variant from Huancayo. My eyes lit up.

The following day at Maltería Market, I spotted a lady with a large bin-shaped pan with what looked like a metal dustbin lid on top. She opened the pan to reveal the most beautiful array of steamed *otongo* buns (p.22), the same that Pamela had told me about the previous night. It was morning – steaming, warm and stuffed with melting *chancaca* syrup, the buns felt like a naughty treat. What better indulgent snack for first thing in the morning? We ate, licked our lips and agreed that our kids would love them.

Deep within the rows of corn-sellers at the market is a half-built building that looks like a small warehouse. The frontage of the shop is narrow, but the room goes back several metres. At the back there are hundreds of sacks of produce. All neatly piled up, one on top of the other, the sacks are like skyscrapers; at their feet are large tubs of every native Peruvian dried ingredient you can think of. I was in awe; like I had found the very heart of Huancayo. In fact, it turned out that this shop is the place where all produce arrives from the region and within a 300-mile radius surrounding it; the place that everyone seems to come to buy. While I stared in wonder, the owners took delivery of sack after sack of ingredients. To me, it felt like every chef's paradise.

I've always loved collecting: Latin and jazz vinyl 45s, black-and-white photos of Peruvian people eating, cookery books from around the world – and this shop was the greatest treat of my year. I picked up handfuls of small sample bags and started filling them. Labelling each bag in turn, Dave and I talked about the ingredients. There were 22 varieties of corn, six varieties of quinoa, four of maca, several of amaranth, 16 of bean and several of pea. There were flours in everything from quinoa to maca to broad bean, chickpea and more. In more than three hours, with a smile on my face at every second, I filled and labelled some 82 small bags of culinary treasure.

Elated, I headed for lunch at the family-run restaurant Huancahuasi. This place has won a national award for its Papa a la Huancaína, an iconic regional dish named not after the province, but after a dazzling lady from Huancayo. Many years ago, when the train line from Lima to neighbouring Cerro de Pasco was being built, women would sell potatoes with different sauces to the men digging out the mountains. One of these ladies was known simply as 'La Huancaína' – a lady from Huancayo. Beautiful and coquettish, she blended white *queso fresco* with cooked hot rocoto pepper, then added milk. She poured the sauce over some boiled potatoes and topped off the snack with a sliced boiled egg. The road diggers used to say that '*La Papa de la Huancaína*' ('The Potato of the Huancayo lady') was the best – and so the dish was named. I tried Huancahuasi's version and it didn't disappoint. The result was creamy and lumpy, and I could tell it had been blended by hand using the traditional *batán*, which gave it an earthy texture.

The restaurant's Huallpa Chupe (p.159) and Pesque de Quinua (p.144) were exquisite, too, and I ate and chatted to owners Doña Esther and Don César Palacios about their 43-year-old restaurant. They told me that the secret to being Huancayo's best restaurant is Mama Lucha – Esther's late mother and keeper of all recipes. I am in awe of restaurateurs who have run restaurants for many years – and 43 years is a long time, especially considering how tough running a business is in Peru. To succeed, Esther and César had treated the restaurant like their home. Their team was their family; their processes had become a culture in itself, a labour of love and discipline. Their passion is deeply inspiring to me: I dream of having a restaurant that succeeds for so long.

Later, back at my hotel I jotted down all the tips they had given me on how to survive in the restaurant business no matter what life throws at you. My to-do list is massive; I shall be implementing it for years to come – and I shall celebrate and think of them, Mama Lucha and all the wonderful *picanteras*, when I, too, maybe reach my 43rd anniversary as chef and restaurateur.

GLOSSARY OF REGIONAL RECIPES

The following recipes are the traditional recipes that come from the regions featured in the book. Those marked with an asterisk (*) are recipes that in truth you might find in more than one of the Andina regions, but for the sake of balance in the book, or because I have a particular association with that recipe in a particular region, here it appears specifically attributed.

APURÍMAC

Yawar Picante* (p.28)
Kapchi de Setas (p.152)
Chochoca* (p.164)
Ponche de Arguedas (p.194)

AREQUIPA

Ocopa Arequipeña & Raíces (p.41)
Torrejas de Sachaca (p.47)
Sarza de Patitas (p.61)
Solterito (p.66)
Sarza de Criadillas (p.68)
Sivinche (p.76)
Celador de Camarones (p.85)
Rocoto Relleno Vegetariano (p.107)
Chupe de Camarones Antiguo (p.160)
Helado de Queso (p.181)
Chicha* (p.199)

AYACUCHO

Puka Picante (p.92)
Cuy Frito* (p.101)
Adobo Ayacuchano (p.143)
Humitas (p.187)

CAJAMARCA

Tamal de Sabogal (p.25)
Caldo Verde de Cajamarca* (p.154)
Caldo de Cabeza* (p.162)

CUSCO

Olluquito con Charqui* (p.104)
Alcachofa a la Parrilla (p.121)
Conejo al Palo (p.130)
Picante de Tarwi (p.147)
Homenaje al Mate de Coca (p.194)

HUANCAVELICA

Patasca de Feli (p.158)
El Puchero* (p.167)

HUÁNUCO

Tacacho con Setas y Beterraga (p.96)
Chaufa Huánuco (p.108)

JUNÍN

Otongo (p.22)
Papa a la Huancaína (p.51)
Ceviche de Alcachofas (p.87)
Trucha a la Parrilla de La Oroya (p.116)
Pastel de Alcachofas (p.118)
Espárragos a la Parrilla (p.133)
Pesque de Quinua (p.144)
Chupe de Olluco (p.157)
Huallpa Chupe (p.159)
Gelatina de Pata (p.185)
Helado de Saúco (p.188)

LA LIBERTAD

Ceviche de Tarwi* (p.77)
Shambar con Chicharrón (p.98)
El Lechóncito de Mamita Naty (p.125)
Guiso de Cabrito de Santiago (p.142)
Higos con Crema de Vainilla (p.177)

PASCO

Pachamanca* (p.109)
Shtrukala de Oxapampa (p.190)

PUNO

Causa Puno (p.58)
Sango con Adobo de Pato (p.138)
Locro de Zapallo (p.140)
Picante de Lengua (p.146)
Chairo de Chambi* (p.165)

RECOMMENDED RESTAURANTS AND PICANTERÍAS IN THE ANDINA REGIONS OF PERU

APURÍMAC

El Pisonay
La Cabañita
Pulpo Pol
Scencias

AREQUIPA

La Capitana
La Cau Cau
La Lucila
La Mundial
La Nueva Palomino

AYACUCHO

La Casona
Maraycha
Recreo Las Flores
Villa La Estancia
Wayrana

CAJAMARCA

El Mirador de Callacpuma
El Zarco
La Campiña
Salas

CUSCO

Ayasqa
El Muro
La Chomba
La Wally
Quinta Eulalia

HUANCAVELICA

Chifa Centro
El Arado
Joy Campestre

HUÁNUCO

Club Campestre Yacutoma
El Bambú Recreo Turístico
Recreo Falcón
Recreo La Perricholi
Rinconcito Huanuqueño

JUNÍN

El Leopardo
Huancahuasi
La Tullpa
Valle Azul

LA LIBERTAD

Batán Mochero
Chanchacapino
El Mochica
La Cazuela
Mi Camote

PASCO

El Típico Pozucino
La Casa de Baco
Rinconcito Oxapampino

PUNO

Balcones de Puno
Kankacho Ayavireño Doña Julia
La Choza de Oscar
La Red Chicharroneria
Mareas, Ceviche y Más